Amish
Peace

Amish
Peace

Simple Wisdom *for*
a Complicated World

Suzanne Woods Fisher

Revell

a division of Baker Publishing Group
Grand Rapids, Michigan

Published by Revell
a division of Baker Publishing Group
P.O. Box 6287, Grand Rapids, MI 49516-6287
www.revellbooks.com

Printed in the United States of America

Library of Congress Cataloging-in-Publication Data
Fisher, Suzanne Woods.
    Amish peace : simple wisdom for a complicated world / Suzanne Woods Fisher.
        p.   cm.
    Includes bibliographical references (p   ).
    ISBN 978-0-8007-3338-4 (pbk.)
    1. Peace—Religious aspects—Amish. 2. Amish—Doctrines. I. Title.
BT736.4.F53 2009
261.8′7308828973—dc22   2009019009

Unless otherwise indicated, Scripture is taken from the HOLY BIBLE, NEW INTER-NATIONAL VERSION®. NIV®. Copyright © 1973, 1978, 1984 by International Bible Society. Used by permission of Zondervan. All rights reserved.

Scripture marked KJV is taken from the King James Version of the Bible.

Scripture marked NLT is taken from the Holy Bible, New Living Translation, copyright © 1996, 2004. Used by permission of Tyndale House Publishers, Inc., Wheaton, Illinois 60189. All rights reserved.

To protect the privacy of those who have shared their stories with the author, some details and names have been changed.

To my grandfather, Wilbur D. Benedict, born a Dunkard (Old Order German Baptist Brethren), who started his career teaching at Pigeon Hole, a one-room schoolhouse in Franklin County, Pennsylvania, and ended it as publisher of *Christianity Today* magazine in its early years. His life inspired me to become a writer.

Contents

Contents

Acknowledgments

I am indebted to the works of John Hostetler and Donald Kraybill and to the people I met in Pennsylvania and Ohio, without whom this book could not have been written. Individuals like Lee and Anita Troup, Don and Elaine Smoot, David Kline, Susie Riehl, Esther Smucker, Erik Wesner, Joel Kime, Dr. Ervin Stutzman, Glenda Lehman Ervin of Lehman's Hardware, and Annie Schar of Annie's Baskets. A special thank-you to Nyna Dolby, friend extraordinaire, for making the time to come with me on an initial trip to Amish America, taking copious notes and pictures. My great appreciation to Joyce Hart, my agent, blessed with the art of making connections. And to editor Andrea Doering, gifted with keen insight.

Throughout this work, proper names, place names, and identifying details have been changed to ensure the privacy of those involved. A few gave permission to use their names. My goal has been to present true stories of the Amish in a way that honors their heritage. If there are any blunders, they are mine. I am grateful to all of the kind Amish people who shared their stories with me. That is the one thing that has stood out for me: the Amish are extraordinarily kind. They go out of their way to help you.

It's easy to get distracted by the buggies and beards, but the Amish aren't all that different from us. As artist Susie Riehl said, "People think the Amish are perfect. We're not. We're the same as anybody. We all need the Lord." At its ideal, the Amish way of life does seem closer to the heart of Christianity, emphasizing tenets of our faith that really matter. Tenets—like turning the other cheek, loving our neighbors, living simply so others may simply live—we may be in danger of neglecting.

It seems the Plain People, in many ways, are not so plain after all.

Introduction

Become Amish?

Do you feel peace—true, inner peace—only in spurts? I do.

My faith is very important to me. I love the Lord, I pray often, I study the Bible, but still, peace of mind often eludes me.

Why is that? Am I missing something? Jesus made a promise to give believers an abiding peace. "Peace I leave with you; my peace I give you. I do not give to you as the world gives. Do not let your hearts be troubled and do not be afraid" (John 14:27).

So why is it that peace often feels elusive, like trying to package fog?

Clearly, Jesus indicates that the peace he offers is different from that which believers can find in the world. Christ meant for our hearts to be anchored in peace. Set firmly in place. Unyielding.

Yet for me, and maybe for you, peace is fleeting, not a constant state of mind.

Perhaps the reason is that I rely on the *wrong* kind of peace—one that is based on circumstances in life all lining up properly, like ducks in a row, which is seldom. Jesus' peace means my heart should not be troubled. But, often, I do feel troubled. Especially when "what-ifs?" bounce like popcorn in my mind. Jesus' peace means that I shouldn't be afraid. But, often, I do fear the future. Lying in bed at night, staring up at the ceiling, I know that no household is entirely safe from natural disaster, fire or theft, stock market crashes or personal suffering. The world, even in a best-case scenario, can only offer a troubled peace.

The truth is that bad things do happen, despite our best efforts to stay safe. There is no guarantee for total security in any area of life. That's why "peace as the world gives" doesn't offer staying power.

The only people I have ever known who seem to have a handle on abiding peace are my relatives, members of the Dunkard Brethren Church. Similar to the Amish but not as strict or as isolated, my Dunkard cousins embody Christ's instruction to "live in the world but not of it." They wear plain, modest clothing, with their trademark bonnets and horseshoe beards, and live in colonies scattered around the country.

The roots of the Anabaptist movement reach back to sixteenth-century Europe. A group of religious radicals rejected the common practice of infant baptism and, instead, affirmed an adult's "believer's baptism." Descendants of the Anabaptist movement are known as the Amish, Mennonites, Hutterites, Church of the Brethren, and Brethren in Christ.

A common element among these groups is their emphasis on developing character, honoring God, avoiding temptation and sin, and living plain. But the peaceful countenance of the Anabaptists runs much deeper than living a simple lifestyle.

There was a time when my cousin Doug and his wife, Mina, sought treatment at Stanford University for their little boy, born with a genetic defect. Since we lived close to the hospital, Doug and Mina stayed with my family now and then. Their peace of mind never wavered, carrying them through the slow and sad death of their firstborn child. They grieved, to be sure, but held confidence in God's sovereignty. Even as a teenager, I sensed I was witnessing something extraordinary.

The Anabaptist communities may seem old-fashioned, but when it comes to living with an abiding peace, they are far beyond most of us living a frazzled, fast-paced modern life.

So is the answer to living with an abiding peace to "go Amish"? Some think so.

An Amish newspaper ran a story about the hundreds of letters they received asking how to become Amish. The article explained that most people wanted a change of pace or were feeling stressed by their hectic lifestyle. The solution, they thought, was to become Amish.

The newspaper conjectured that most likely, they wouldn't last a day in the Amish lifestyle. One cold winter ride in a buggy would send them scurrying to get home, happy to flip on the car heater and switch on the radio.

"Uncle Amos," an Amish man who wrote occasionally for the *Small Farmer's Journal*, wrote this thought-provoking response:

Become Amish?

If you admire our faith, strengthen yours. If you admire our sense of commitment, deepen yours. If you admire our community spirit, build your own. If you admire the simple life, cut back. If you admire deep character and enduring values, live them yourself.[1]

We don't need to "go Amish" to bring true peace into our lives. In fact, it's nearly impossible to become Amish. There is a basic foundation of being Amish, called *Gelassenheit*, that is simply contrary to the American way of thinking. *Gelassenheit* is translated to mean "yielding to a higher authority." The Amish believe in living a life of humility and submission to God, as well as the church district's leaders and *Ordnung* (rules for living). It's more than just living without conveniences; the welfare of the community is at the forefront of decision making. It means that drawing attention to oneself is inappropriate—very different from our tendency to be considered special. It means keeping life simple so they can emphasize what is truly important.

But peace? The lasting peace we long for isn't exclusive to the Amish. Their example is our example. Their principles can be our principles. Their peace, based in the security of God, can belong to us too.

But . . . how?

Amish Peace: Simple Wisdom for a Complicated World seeks to answer that question by exploring the taproot of the Amish. We can graft into it—an "English" tree drawing strength from Amish roots—and integrate those principles into our modern life.

Plain and simple, a troubled heart is not Jesus' intent for you, or me. A heart anchored in peace is.

Part 1

Simplicity

Take all you want, eat all you take.

Amish Proverb

By the cash register at my favorite coffee shop sits a stack of business cards that promise to simplify my life. The secret, shouts the card, is to "Get Organized!" A worthy goal, but I have a feeling that its aim is to help me stuff even more activities into my weighted-with-responsibilities schedule—not exactly my definition of simple living. Actually, I'm not sure any of us in the twenty-first century—running breathless, addicted to technologies that are supposed to make our lives easier but really make them far more complex—well, I'm not sure any of us *get* what simple living really means.

Except for, maybe, the Amish.

The Amish personify simple living. To the casual observer, their life of simplicity seems based on living with less choice. When an Amish woman wakes in the morning, she doesn't face countless decisions about how to carry on with her day: what to wear, what to do, how to do it. It's already been decided: Friday? housecleaning; Saturday? grass cutting; Monday? laundry day. She knows exactly what has to be done and in what order.

But having less choice isn't what makes the Amish life a simple life. A truly simple life is much more than that.

There's a verse in the Bible that keeps rolling around in my mind. Jesus tells his listeners not to lay up for themselves treasures on earth, where rust and moth can attack (Matt. 6:19–21). I know there's a layer of eternity in Jesus' words, but I think there's also a very practical, earthly application in those verses. Rust and moth only attack things that are neglected. Forgotten. Devalued.

In fact, I've wondered if Jesus' remark was inspired by a memory of some Nazareth neighbor's overflowing garage. Neighbors like mine, who pay monthly storage locker fees to store things that they seldom use, so that rust and moth can settle in, undisturbed, for a feast.

Do you feel overwhelmed by clutter in your life? I sure do—both figuratively and literally. Peace of mind vanishes when I feel overwhelmed. In its place swarm restlessness and fretting, as if I'm wearing a pair of pants that are one size too small. I'm just not comfortable. That feeling happens whenever I let nonessentials crowd out the essentials. My treasures—time with the Lord, time with my family—get shoved to the back of the attic, gathering dust, while less important things—an endless to-do list, projects that seem essential but probably aren't—grab my full attention.

The Amish have a guiding principle that seems to rest on Jesus' words: to *only* live with things that they really use. And to treasure them.

In the Amish world—and applicable to our world—Jesus' principle extends to more than material objects. It relates to guarding well what the Amish truly treasure: their families, their homes, their communities, their faith.

That's what keeps life simple.

The Worth of Money

He who has no money is poor; he who has nothing but money is even poorer.

Amish Proverb

When David and Elsie Kline started *Farming* magazine in 2001, David described the experience as going off the end of a dock in a cannonball dive. "I didn't know how deep the water would be," David said. Committed to farming in harmony with nature, David knew there was a need for a farm magazine that really cared about small-scale farming. The Klines had a vision of a literate quarterly dedicated to teaching others, Amish and non-Amish, about how they can make a good living from a small farm, the old-fashioned way: without heavy machines or pesticides, and in ways that welcome wildlife. "We wanted to be the voice of hope for small farmers," he explained.

They faced a few obstacles that would have buckled the faint of heart: David and Elsie did not have any money with which to start a magazine. They would have to do it while they continued to farm for a living. The Klines live on a farm in Holmes County, Ohio. Although David had written for magazines, including *National Wildlife*, and had published two books, he had no experience in publishing a magazine. Like most Old Order Amish, David's formal education stopped at the eighth grade, though his edification certainly didn't stop there. An anonymous private grant had been donated to Holmes County, earmarked for vocational training for those with an eighth-grade education. "It wasn't government money," David was quick to point out. "It was private money." The Amish reject any government subsidies or benefits, like Social Security. Even a government grant would be viewed as a "handout." David applied for and was awarded the grant; that seed money produced the first issue of 5,000 copies. *Farming* magazine has been self-supporting ever since.

David and Elsie believe passionately in a kind of farming that is done out of reverence for nature as part of God's divine creation. Farming for profit, including the production of *Farming* magazine, is secondary. Working hard for the principles they stand for and live by, not for money and accumulation of wealth, is an Amish core value. "Money is there to help others," said David. "Not to get rich. It's a little ironic. Even though we Amish have a work ethic that can eventually accumulate wealth, we believe in restricting wealth." He gave a short laugh. "We don't have anything like a Lexus buggy."

David told a story about a technician who advised him to join the no-till crowd and be freed from plowing. That way, the fellow reasoned, David and his sons could work in a factory. The technician assumed that the extra income would improve the quality of the Klines' lives. "What's to improve?" David asked. "Besides, I like to plow." He plows with horses, rather than a tractor, to avoid compacting the soil. An added bonus: when the horses rest, he can read.

The Klines have forty-five Jersey dairy cows that support two families—theirs, plus their daughter and son-in-law. David describes the Jersey as the cow for the dairyman who likes to read. Jerseys tend to be low-maintenance, intelligent, carefree animals. "We'll never get wealthy," he said, "but we're supporting ourselves."

That suits the Klines just fine. Worrying about money isn't something David and Elsie are inclined to do. After seven years, the magazine seems to have found a loyal audience; its spine grows thicker with every issue. "I've edited *Farming* for seven years without pay," he said. "We like to use the money to pay the writers. We have good writers from all over."

The Klines aren't particularly worried about the long-term viability of the magazine. They believe that if God wants the magazine to continue, it will. If not, well, they hope it did some good while it lasted.

One of David's brothers, a minister in the Amish church since 1959, often quotes a verse in the book of Proverbs: "Give me neither poverty nor riches; feed me with food convenient for me; lest I be full, and deny thee, and say, Who is the LORD? or lest I be poor, and steal, and take the name of my God in vain " (30:8–9 KJV). "That's where I aim to be with money," David said. He spoke with gentleness, conviction, and a twinkle in his eye. "Just enough for today and not a penny more."

Reflections on Simplicity

David and Elsie Kline decided to invest in something they felt had value. Yet they were equally comfortable letting it go if God did not provide enough for it to continue. What's your perspective on things you value? Do they mean more than they should?

How would you define a successful life? Have you ever asked yourself, "What does that definition of success cost me?"

How often do you worry about money?

Ask God to illuminate your understanding of how living simply can bring about his peace.

PLAIN *Living*

Less than 5 percent of all new Amish businesses fail—the national average for small-business failures exceeds 65 percent.[1]

Small-Scale Living

We live simply so others may simply live.

Amish Proverb

R ay Miller, a barrel-chested man with a ruddy complexion and a broad smile, grew up on the land he now farms. So did his father, and his grandfather, and his great-grandfather. "It didn't look then like it does now," says Ray. "My great-grandfather bought it at a bargain because no one else wanted it. It was pretty rocky and untillable."

The human urge to improve any patch of ground is strong, especially true for the Amish. The early Anabaptists lived in remote areas in Europe, on land no one could farm. They tilled the soil and improved it, an enduring Amish characteristic. Looking out over the rolling fields, pungent with the aroma of freshly turned earth, Ray might have understated his ancestors' energies. This land is not only priceless, it is clearly cherished.

When Ray married, his father sold the farm to him and retired. "Dad still helps out a lot, though," Ray says. "I don't think he could ever stay out of the fields. We ask his advice for just about everything." He stops suddenly to clear his throat, trying to hide the fact that he is choking up. Sheepishly, he adds, "I get a little emotional about it. Growing up here, you're part of a legacy."

Even though Ray can afford it, he has no plan to add more tillable acres. "Why?" he asks, shrugging his big shoulders. "We couldn't take care of more. With this size farm there is usually something to do, without being overwhelmed."

Few Amish farms have more than eighty tillable acres. They traditionally maintain a scale of farming that enables each farm to be worked by a family. The use of horses to do field work automatically limits the expansion and size of farms. Even still, during harvest times, with all hands on deck, family labor is not enough. Help from the neighbors is required. "One year," says Ray, "we had more third-cutting hay than we needed, so we made a deal with a neighbor who needed more hay. He got the extra hay and in turn he let us borrow his bull to, ahem . . ." Ray turns a shade of plum. "To visit with a few lady cows." Farming, old-fashioned style.

From the size of their farms to the size of their churches, staying small suits the Amish. Each church district is kept to roughly twenty to thirty families. It's a size that accommodates everyone in one house but is still small enough for everyone to know each other's names. When a district grows too large, it will split and form another.

There's a big "for sale" sign hanging at the farm next to Ray's. Isn't he tempted, just a little, to buy it? After all, someday he might have a son of his own. He shakes his head. "Never even gave it a thought. Maybe I would, if I had a son or two. But for now, I'm just trying to take care of what I got." He stands up and stretches, ready to head out to the barn to feed the animals. "I always say, my great-grandfather started this farm, my grandfather improved it. My father improved it more." Ray gives a big toothy grin. "My job is not to mess it up."

With all Ray's heart, he believes that the exact ways his ancestors did things are more than good enough for him. Ray's farm is nothing big, nothing splashy. But enough to get the job done nicely. "Just a small, well-cared-for farm to pass on to my son." And, in doing so, get it ready for the next couple of hundred years.

REFLECTIONS ON SIMPLICITY

The Amish believe that setting limits on almost everything is one of the foundations of wisdom. Have you ever thought about setting limits on your lifestyle? If so, what kind of limits?

Amish leaders try to help church members avoid temptation. They take temptations very seriously. Examine your lifestyle. What are you pursuing? Does it have eternal value? Are you seeking things above or earthly things? Is it drawing you closer to God or keeping you from him?

Most of us find it hard to live within our means. How well do you do? Do you think you would experience greater peace if you lived within your means? If so, what needs to change?

PLAIN *Living*

A research report from Ohio State University Extension agent Randy James, who works in the Amish country of Geauga County, Ohio, found that net income on an Amish farm can be ten times higher per acre than on a modern, high-tech farm.[2]

Family First

It's better to have a wife on your team than on your back.

Amish Proverb

Sarah Lehman is a tiny slip of a woman in her late forties who moves with the energy of a teenager. Her blond hair is covered with a bandanna handkerchief knotted at the nape of her neck below the bun. On her slim feet are flip-flops. Sarah has six children, ranging in age from twenty-one down to five-year-old twins. Her eyes, as blue as delft plates, reveal the kind of serene countenance that makes one think a three-ring circus could be going on around her and she would remain quiet and unflustered. With all of Sarah's responsibilities, she still finds time to help her children as they play or visit with a friend who drops by.

A few years ago, Sarah and her husband, Abel, bought a booth at the Central Market in Lancaster in hopes of supplementing their farm income. "We sold salads," she explained. "Most of the salads were ordered, but the coleslaw we made right there, fresh. We couldn't make enough of it. Customers realized it was fresh, watched us while we were cutting it up, and poof!" She snapped her fingers. "It was gone!"

Abel, a man with an entrepreneurial streak and a sense of what his customers wanted, decided it was time to branch out. "One day," Sarah said, eyebrows knitted together in a frown, "Abel told me he didn't order potato salad this week. He wanted me to make it. But I'd never made potato salad in my life!" She shook her head, amazed. "So I looked for a recipe. I tried it with the yellow potatoes, and people liked it. Then I tried a German recipe with the red-skinned variety. People liked that too, so we offered both."

With hands on her hips, Sarah said, "Next thing I know, Abel tells me that he didn't order macaroni salad. So I try making a macaroni salad recipe. Then, another week, he told me he didn't order chocolate pudding. That's when I put my foot down. I told him, 'No! I don't make chocolate pudding.' Abel went on up to his mother's house to see if she made it, but she told him she didn't make it either." She laughed. "So he had to order the pudding, after all."

The booth became so profitable that Abel ended up being away from home three to four days a week. Sarah put her foot down on that too. "I tried to keep the kids awake, but they fell asleep on the floor, waiting for their dad," she said. "Finally, I told him, this is no way to raise a family, with Dad gone."

Abel agreed that they needed to make a change. He didn't like spending so much time away from home, either. "He's as much a part of the children growing up as I am as a mother," Sarah said. "So he sold the booth. We decided to build a commercial kitchen on the property. We hired three to four Amish workers who come in every day to make the salads. Now we sell my salads all over the place, as far away as Baltimore."

It's clear that Sarah is a full partner to Abel's business ventures. Many women operate small businesses in their homes. Some even employ their husbands.

Though women do not serve as ordained leaders in the Amish church, they have a voice and a vote in church business meetings.

"Women are very much involved in worship services," said one Old Order Amish bishop. "Since our church is in homes, the women actually have a lot to do in preparation for the service. I think it's a good thing, because they end up sharing the role."

It would be easy to presume that because the Amish have a patriarchal hierarchy, women are oppressed. Young Amish girls do not have the choices that other girls face. Girls grow up to become wives and mothers, keep house, and raise children. A girl is taught the skills of becoming a "housewife" early in life—not such easy tasks when one lives without refrigeration or electricity. Single women, as well as bachelors, lack status in the family-oriented community. A bachelor cannot hold a church office, for example.

But in a society that greatly esteems marriage and motherhood, tremendous value and respect is placed on women and their roles. The home is central to the Amish way of life, and the mother is the heart of every home.

Reflections on Simplicity

One English woman, friendly with many Amish families, said that she has never seen an Amish woman belittle her husband. "There might be good-natured teasing," she said, "but never mean-spiritedness, never critical." Today, commit to practicing the same in your marriage.

Sarah places a high value on the role she plays in her family. Does she put motherhood in a new light for you?

Sarah put her foot down on Abel's work hours because her priority was what was best for her family. When facing a choice, the Amish hold it up against their priorities, then make their decision. How does that simplify decision making?

God's Spirit often guides us by giving us a lack of peace about a certain direction. Have you ever experienced that? How did you resolve it to restore peace?

What can you limit to allow for greater peace in your life?

PLAIN *Living*

While Amish girls learn early to harness the horses and drive buggies, they don't generally own their own buggies unless they remain unmarried. Young women receive trousseaus of dishes, linen, and furniture.[3]

Amish Stuff

Trickles tend to become streams, and streams become torrents.

Amish Proverb

Ella Troyer tried to ignore that familiar but uncomfortable gnawing in the pit of her stomach when she put the "Crafts for Sale" sign up on her front lawn. A year ago, she and her husband, Zeke, had started a sideline business to sell handmade crafts. They needed the income after suffering a blow to their crops from a ruthless summer storm.

But Ella has never been able to quiet her inner battle. It just seemed wrong, she thought, to make Amish dolls for tourists. "I dress plain to avoid attracting attention, to be humble," she told Zeke at breakfast, "so why am I making dolls to attract tourists?" She could never get comfortable with the idea that she was making things she would never use herself. "It bothers me that I might be encouraging worldly people to be even more worldly, to buy things they don't need."

The Amish are thrifty to the point of being labeled parsimonious. One of their cardinal values is to be resourceful, wasting nothing, living in harmony with nature, and recycling virtually . . . everything! Right down to spreading their fields with manure from their livestock to avoid expensive, artificial chemicals. Their houses and barns are Spartan-like, spacious and uncluttered. It's not that they don't have toys for their children and all kinds of Tupperware in the kitchen. They do. But what they have, they need. What they have, they use.

Ella's dilemma is shared by many in the Amish church. Just a few decades ago, Plain People who produced or sold items that were not useful, or used by church members, would have caught the scrutiny of the elders. But on the heels of the economic woes that beset the Amish in the early 1960s came tourism. Lancaster, Pennsylvania, is now one of the country's top tourist attractions. An estimated 8.3 million tourists visit annually and spend more than $1.5 billion. Almost all Plain communities in the United States have seen an upsurge in tourism.

With tourism came opportunities—to create revenue, to maintain farms and the way of life they hold dear. Many, like Ella and Zeke, erect roadside stands or home-based shops from which they sell quilts, crafts, wooden birdhouses, farm produce, and so forth. Those sideline businesses are not only enterprising but downright prosperous.

If Amish souls are troubled by tourists, they don't show it. They move about and quietly mind their own business. This is their world, and if the English come to visit, gaping at them as if they were stage props in a show, choosing to spend their dollars to boost the local economy, so be it.

There are chafing points, though. "It's wrong to use the Amish name to sell something," Zeke said. "You won't see the Amish doing it—it's always the English, trying to increase their business. But it looks like we are using our religion to sell our products." Ella's prayer cap strings bobbed, as if keeping time, as she nodded in agreement with Zeke. In a touch of irony, one large box store on Route 30 calls itself "Amish Stuff."

And aside from the inflow of cash into the local economy, the very presence of curious tourists affirms the Plain way of life. They are telling the Amish that they have something worth keeping.

REFLECTIONS ON SIMPLICITY

What do you think of Ella's opinion that Christians should only be buying things they need, rather than things they want?

Look around the room where you are right now. What is gathering dust? Does it have value to you? Think about the things that share your space—are they things you value or do they hinder what really matters in life?

How would you describe simple living? Fewer possessions? Fewer choices? Or what about an emphasis on only the things that really matter?

If you had a few spare hours, how would you spend it? Your answer indicates what you really treasure. How can you better guard your treasure?

PLAIN *Living*

For many reasons, the Amish have an aversion to having their picture taken. The original reason is unclear, but the taboo has been legitimatized, said Donald B. Kraybill, a nationally recognized scholar on Anabaptist groups and a professor at Elizabethtown College in Pennsylvania, by stating the Second Commandment that there shall not be any graven images. Assertive tourists snap pictures anyway. It's really quite ironic: a group of people who wish not to be photographed are perhaps the most photographed ethnic group in America.

The Amish Dress Code

The most beautiful attire is a smile.

Amish Proverb

Edith Hochstetler, at ninety, sits hunchbacked in her favorite chair as she stares out the front window. Her spine is curved like a question mark. A starched organza prayer cap covers her sparse hair twisted tightly back into a bun. Edith's skin is lined with wrinkles and brown spots, her teeth worn and yellowed. But in her milky blue eyes, there is a depth of contentment that nearly makes her glow.

Edith's clothing is the traditional garb of an Old Order Amish woman—a long-sleeved, dark blue dress covered by a black apron that falls just below her knees. Most Amish women make their own dresses, buying fabric from local dry goods stores and stitching them on treadle machines. Her dress and apron are held together with a row of severe, long straight pins down her chest. Yes, you read that right. Straight pins—not safety pins, not kilt skirt pins. Don't they poke? "Oh no," Edith answers, laughing, patting her thin chest. "You get used to them."

"May not seem like it to the English, but there have always been changes to our dress," Edith continued, rocking forward in her chair to speak. "There's a story my grandmother used to tell from the days of Jesse James. He cut his frock coat back to get to his guns faster. This started to become the style for everybody's frock coats. Even the Amish were cutting their *mutzis* (black coats) back too. But then the bishops got to worrying; said it was worldly. So they made a rule." She stops to catch her breath before continuing. "About that time, Abe Lincoln stovepipe hats were all in style. Tall hats started showing up in church. So the bishops made a rule. The crown of the hat could be no more than five inches. Those rules stick." She laughs. "Until something new comes up."

Distinctive clothing has been part of the Anabaptist movement dating back to its very beginning in the 1500s. Historical development of dress has been traced to the type of clothing worn by peasants in Germany, Holland, France, and Switzerland. The Anabaptists adopted plain styles of dress and conduct as a means of protest against the nobility who oppressed them. The nobles wore powdered wigs, fancy buttons, elegant coats, trousers for the men, elaborate gowns for the women.

Simple dress and grooming continue to be important symbols of Amish unity and community. Like a uniform, their clothes promote equality rather than pride or status.

The simple grooming of the Amish carries symbolism too. The men and boys wear their hair straight, not "shingled" (layered), and long enough to cover their earlobes. Men grow beards after marriage, untrimmed. No mustaches, though. Big bushy mustaches were a popular fashion in the European military. It's common to see many elderly Amish women with a balding part on their pink scalp, like Edith's. Her hair has been parted down the middle and twisted back from the crown since she was a toddler—as soon as it was long enough to be gathered into a tight bun. Edith's hair has never been cut. Not once.

"When I get dressed in the morning," Edith said, "I don't have to think about what to wear. I don't have to fiddle away time with silly choices. When I pin my apron, I remind myself that I belong to God and I belong to the Amish." She smiled, crinkling the sun creases around her eyes. "My clothes tell me that, every day."

REFLECTIONS ON SIMPLICITY

What does your clothing express about you?

How much time is spent on your clothing needs? How much of it is on your clothing wants? What's the difference?

Amish clothing is symbolic, a tangible reminder of a person's choice to be a baptized member of the Amish church. What are ways we can remind ourselves that we belong to God?

PLAIN *Living*

An Amish woman uses about a dozen straight pins to fasten the bodice of her dress and the apron over it.[4]

A Love Affair with Scooters

How fast the wheel of change is spinning.

Amish Proverb

L ined up in a bicycle rack in front of a barn at an Amish farm
is a row of scooters in various sizes and colors—red, blue,
and green. Around four o'clock in the afternoon, Simon
Bontrager went looking for his five-year-old son, Reuben, finding
him high up in a treehouse perched over a stream. Simon cupped
his mouth to holler up the tree, "Hey, Rube! Come on down. We
gotta make a run to the village store for Mom. She's missing an
ingredient for her dessert."

Reuben popped his head over the edge of the tree house and
peered down at his father. "What for?" he asked.

"Cinnamon."

Reuben's eyes went wide. *"Apfelschnitz?"*

Simon nodded, grinning as his son scrambled down the tree as
agile as a monkey. Simon unbuckled his leather work belt, full of
tools, and hung it on a hook in the barn. Reuben hurried to pull his
father's large red scooter from the rack. Simon grabbed the handle
and held it steady as Reuben stepped up on the narrow platform.

Simon hopped on and pushed off with one leg, and the two of them practically flew down the hill to the store.

It's been said that the Amish have a love affair with their scooters—a bicycle without pedals. A common sight in Lancaster County is to see Amish men, women, and children using these colorful scooters as transportation, thrusting one foot against the road to build up speed, or coasting down a hill with the wind against their face. It's easy to see they're having fun.

In the 1920s, as bicycles arrived on the scene, Amish church leaders gave the bicycle some serious consideration. "Our fathers and forefathers thought the bicycles with pedals were too modern," explained Simon. "They knew it would be too easy to get too far from home." The home is the heart of Amish life. If a new gizmo poses a threat to that heart, well, say no more. The bicycle was banned.

But then someone engineered a scooter. It wasn't long before nearly every Amish family from Ohio to Maryland had one or two. "The way the story goes," Simon explained, stroking his wiry beard, eyes snapping with good humor, "the bishops got together to talk about banning the scooters. The thing was, they all arrived at the meeting on scooters. So," he said, throwing his hands up in the air, "they voted against the ban."

The acceptance of the scooter reflects an Amish-style "selective modernization." When something new reaches into the Amish community, the church leaders might give it a period of probation, weighing out its long-term effects, and each church district comes to its own conclusions. And, always, the church leaders consider where a change could lead the younger generation. They try to see beyond the immediate benefits of change to the effects it could have down the road. How could this new technology or gadget tempt someone away from the church? Or to disobey God?

"The leaders are wise. They know that there will always be those who push the line," Simon said, eyes smiling. "We're all human.

Amish, Catholic, English. There are always those who can get carried away."

Reflections on Simplicity

The Amish consider the long-term consequences of something new and how it will affect the community's welfare. They appreciate comfort and convenience but realize it's not the ultimate reason for our being here. They make decisions with higher purposes in mind. Before accepting or buying a new technology, have you ever thought, what will this lead to? Consider making today's purchase with your ultimate goals in mind.

Look around your house. How many gadgets do you see that promise to save you time, effort, or money? Have they lived up to their promise?

The Amish have a saying: Once drawn, lines are hard to erase. Where do you draw the line on what technology is acceptable for your family and what isn't? How does recognizing that "line" (or priority) simplify decision making?

PLAIN *Living*

The Amish are never to lose touch with the earth, which is why their buggies' wheel rims and other farm equipment must not be separated from the ground by a rubber cushion.[5]

The Cool Factor

A man is rich in proportion to the things he can afford to leave alone.

Amish Proverb

The winding two-lane country road ends at Viola and Joe Byler's spacious farm, just a few hundred yards down from a light blue telephone shanty. Five generations of Joe's family have farmed these seventy acres of prime, flat farmland in the heart of Lancaster County. The farmhouse sits smack in the center of the acreage. It's typical of Old Order Amish houses—two stories, spreading in all directions the way a family spreads.

On one side of the main house is the *Grossdaadi Haus* (granddaddy house), where Joe's grandmother lived until she passed. Joe's parents live there now. Joe is one of six children, but the only one interested in taking over the farm. When Joe and Viola married, his parents retired and moved from the big house into the Grossdaadi Haus—a graceful rite of passage.

The interior of Joe and Viola's home is simple. Shiny gray linoleum covers the floor, scratched and scuffed but spotless. The walls are painted in a glossy pale green. Even the high ceilings are painted green. The Amish are tidy and sensible housekeepers; it is much easier to wash a glossy paint wall than a flat paint wall. The acceptable paint colors are from nature's palette: blue for the sky, green for the grass, brown for the soil.

The kitchen and family room, the hub of family activity, combine to make a large great room, couch included. It's said that every Amish home has a couch in the kitchen. Partitions separate the rooms and allow for large groups—as many as 150 to 200—to gather for Sunday church, weddings, or funerals. The house is filled with comfortable, mismatched furniture, a little on the shabby side. On the wall is a clock with chimes sounding on the quarter and half hour. Walls are mostly bare, except for picture calendars. A desk in the corner is cluttered, piled with assorted papers, magazines, and the latest copies of *The Budget*, the Amish newspaper. Two woodstoves anchor the corners of the downstairs interior, one at each end, like bookends. It's warm inside, full of the semisweet smell of lantern oil and woodsmoke from the stoves.

"It's the only room that's heated," Viola explains. "At night, the entire family gathers here. Everyone is together. The kids do their homework, Dad reads, I'll be finishing up something in the kitchen."

Wouldn't it be simple to heat the other rooms? Granted, the Amish don't have central heating, but it couldn't be that hard to lug a kerosene heater upstairs so the kids could study quietly. Would it?

The answer comes swiftly.

"No!" Viola says, eyes wide. "We love being together. It's our way. Why, if other rooms were heated, everyone would . . . well, they would scatter!" She says it as if it were a sin.

To the Amish way of thinking, it might be. They safeguard their family time as if a precious commodity. Moments together are to be cherished.

Joe and Viola's home is clearly guided by practicality, not by the latest style trends. It's cozy but outdated, the way your grandmother's house might be. It is well cared for, evokes a pleasant feeling, but is definitely not stylish or "cool."

When you're Amish, it's easy to decide what to wear, how to travel, and how to decorate the house. These choices are guided by the *Ordnung*, an oral tradition, a blueprint that orders the whole way of Amish life, including how to furnish a house. For example, a telephone is not permitted in an Amish home but is permitted to be housed in an outside shanty.

We non-Amish types might object to having a church choose our house paint. The Ordnung seems confining and restrictive, invasive, even. It's true that the Amish are not free to *do* some things. However, they are free *from* many others. They are not free to buy the latest fashions, but they are free from the anxiety of what to wear and free from the habit of recreational shopping. They are not free to buy the latest flat-screen television (or any television, for that matter), but they are free from the influence of television. They are not free to buy the latest car, but they are free from the temptation of purchasing a status symbol, including the debt that goes along with it.

Although Amish women are not free to use makeup on their faces, they are free from the pressure to look "perfect" or to fight normal aging or to be a size 2 when their body wants to be a size 10. The Amish are not free to accept Social Security checks, but they are free from worrying about who will care for them in their old age. They are free from trying to keep up with the Joneses, free from feeling inferior to others, free from competition among friends.

They are free to be uncool.

REFLECTIONS ON SIMPLICITY

A recurring theme in many of our lives is having a lot and wanting more. In what ways do you observe our culture to be a snare to you?

How much of life—even your mental life—gets frittered away with trying to be cool?

Contrast the Amish avoidance of the value of being cool to your own views.

What things in your life seek first place? Why is it important to keep a careful watch on what is mastering our lives?

PLAIN *Living*

The homes of the Swartzentruber Amish and similar groups tend to be the most primitive looking. Metal roofs and dirt lanes are characteristic. Usually Swartzentruber yards are a bit scrabbly looking compared to the typical meticulously-cared-for Old Order front lawn. Some say this may reflect a difference in concern for the material world.[6]

A Word to the Wise

Medicine and advice are two things more pleasant to give than to receive.

Amish Proverb

As Sadie King herded her children—all four talking at once—into the buggy, she said, "*Silent* and *listen* are spelled with the same letters." The children quieted down as they tried to puzzle that out, which was exactly what Sadie had hoped for. She smiled to herself as she slapped the horse's reins to get him trotting. She had promised a neighbor who just had a baby that she would bring dinner to her, and she was running late.

The Amish thread proverbial sayings into everyday speech to teach their children moral lessons. Easy to remember, based in everyday life, proverbs are an ancient and powerful teaching tool, an oral tradition passed through the centuries from times when few were literate.

These time-tested proverbs—such as "God has two dwellings, one in heaven and the other in a meek and thankful heart" or "You can't keep trouble from coming, but you needn't give it a chair to sit on" or "Many things have been opened by mistake, but none so frequently as the mouth"—become like small lights along a path, guiding a child (adults too) toward wise behavior and choices. They have a way of clearing away the gray fog, distilling an issue down to black or white clarity, simplifying the decision. And helping a child remember simple but piercing wisdom.

Sadie told a story about her son Jimmy. When he was four years old, he left a garden trowel out in the yard, where it rusted in the rain. "Instead of just admitting that he forgot to put it away, Jimmy made up a lie about it. He said a burglar had broken into the toolshed and stolen all of the tools. When my husband asked him why only that one trowel was missing, Jimmy said that the burglar felt so bad about stealing from us that he brought everything back. But he dropped the trowel in the yard and didn't notice it."

Sadie couldn't hold back a grin. "His story just got bigger and bigger, more and more complicated, until he finally gave up and confessed the truth. A year later, I overheard Jimmy give some advice to his sister: 'Just tell Mom the truth, Lyddie. One lie brings the next one with it.'" Sadie laughed. "He sounded just like his father! So there's an example where those sayings really do stick and help a child the next time he's tempted."

Proverbs are so much a part of the culture that tourist stores in Amish Country sell plaques with these "Pennsylvania Dutch" witticisms. The contributors to *The Budget* often end their letters with a famous quote or pithy saying they have penned or heard from others.

These Amish proverbs, acting as "rules" of living, also serve as windows into the lives of those private people, revealing what matters most to them. What is important to the Amish? A gentle spirit, pleasing God, hard work, a good character, contentment, caring for the land, living as an example to others.

Sadie steered the horse over to the hitching post, and Jimmy hopped down to tie the reins. The buggy tilted to one side as everyone hopped out. "We're only a little late, Mom," Lyddie said. "But better late than never!"

Sadie picked up the hot casserole with two quilted oven pads and turned to her daughter, one eyebrow arched. "Better never late."

REFLECTIONS ON SIMPLICITY

What are some sayings or proverbs that you grew up with? How did they help remind you to make a better choice or to emphasize a value?

Have you ever stopped to acknowledge the values you want to pass on to your children? How do you do it? Do you try to help your children memorize Bible verses? What about sins you want to avoid, such as gossiping or coveting or losing your temper?

The book of Proverbs in the Bible has all kinds of helpful advice. For example, "A fool gives full vent to his anger, but a wise man keeps himself under control" (Prov. 29:11) or "Without wood a fire goes out; without gossip a quarrel dies down" (Prov. 26:20). Pick a few proverbs from the Bible for your own children to memorize. Write them on an index card and tape them to the refrigerator or the bathroom mirror.

PLAIN *Living*

Whoopie Pies. Legend has it that when Pennsylvania Dutch children would find these traditional cream-cheese-icing-filled chocolate cookie cakes in their lunches, they'd be so excited they'd cry, "Whoopee!"

Slim and Trim

Jumping for joy is good exercise.

Amish Proverb

When Sue Bender, an artist from Berkeley, California, lived with an Amish family to learn about them, she found they wanted to learn about her life too. One day, she described her exercise regimen of walking.

The family burst out laughing at her.

The Amish don't really exercise. That is to say, exercise is not a separate activity in their life. A recent study in *Medicine & Science in Sports & Exercise* researched a southern Ontario Canadian Amish settlement. The conservative Amish, known for living without modern technology and conveniences, utilized nineteenth-century farming techniques that require physical labor. Researchers decided that their lifestyle would give an idea of how North Americans used to live, in a pre-industrialized society, compared to the physical requirements of modern-day living.[7]

Ninety-eight Amish adults in a southern Ontario farming community agreed to wear pedometers and log their physical activities for seven days. The results of the study indicated that a very high level of physical activity was integrated into the daily lives of the Amish. Not a huge surprise but it did confirm the scientists' hunches.

Then they compared that level of activity to an average modern English adult. That's where jaws dropped in surprise. Researchers found that an Old Order Amish adult was six times more active than an average English adult. Six times! Amish men, who mostly work as farmers, reported an average of ten hours of vigorous work per week and took an average of 18,425 steps a day. One man recorded more than 51,000 steps in a single day—walking behind a team of horses while plowing. Women, reporting moderate forms of activity such as gardening, cooking, and childcare, still achieved an average of 14,196 daily steps.

Another unexpected finding was that only 4 percent of the Amish were considered obese despite a diet dense in calories and carbohydrates. The typical Amish diet is based on a Swiss-German preference for dumplings, potatoes, gravy, fried foods, and sugary desserts. Ever tried a whoopie pie? Or stewed saltine crackers? Or marshmallow peanut butter on white bread? Carbohydrate heaven! Amish women are known as good cooks. Every community gathering is embellished with an abundance of food. And yet Amish adults were able to maintain a more ideal body weight through physical activity.

The Amish exercise study highlighted the importance of physical activity. It was able to show just how far, in levels of physical activity, North Americans have fallen in the last 150 years or so, resulting in a modern obesity epidemic. An even more recent study of Lancaster Amish by *Archives of Internal Medicine* found that three to four hours of moderate physical activity—walking briskly, gardening, running after children—overrode a genetic predisposition to obesity.[8] Just getting up and moving.

Sometimes, it seems, we need fancy studies to tell us obvious things.

Reflections on Simplicity

How should we view the world's approach to exercise? What is the ultimate goal? To live longer? To look younger? To stay healthier? To maintain a weight?

The benefits of exercise go far beyond losing weight or strengthening muscle. Exercise eliminates anxiety, boosts the immune system, gets blood flowing to the brain, reduces the risk for Alzheimer's disease, allows for relaxation, and improves peace of mind. Something as simple as a daily walk enhances the quality of one's life. Said one health counselor, "You can't find a better stress reliever than physical exercise."

How do worry and anxiety spill over into your daily life? Regular exercise, good nutrition, and adequate rest are simple ways to promote peace and defuse anxiety in your life. Simple ways to simply live. Today, take good care of your body. Be mindful to see if it helps you attain greater peace of mind.

PLAIN *Living*

The family garden is an important and cooperative enterprise. Some families preserve up to 800 quarts of fruits and vegetables each year.[9]

Off the Grid

Use it up, wear it out, make it do, or do without.

Amish Proverb

As the storm came through and the sky blackened, Alva Fisher hurried inside with a basket of freshly air-dried laundry. She lit the lamp hanging from a hook in the ceiling in her kitchen. The stark white light illuminated the whole room, bouncing shadows off of her shiny linoleum floor. Brighter than most gas lamps, it did not make the usual hissing sounds that come from a pressure gas lamp. "It's a solar-powered electric lamp," Alva explained. "It's powered by a solar cell in the backyard." She went over to the window and pointed to the fencepost, where the solar cell was fastened. "Even on a cloudy day like today, there's enough sunlight for the lamp to work."

Alva's husband, Menno, has used solar energy for years—the fencing around their dairy farm is electric, powered by solar electricity. The Amish were among the first to explore solar electricity and adapt it to farming. Surprised? Most think of the Amish as living a nineteenth-century life—before the days of public utility companies.

The Amish did turn their back on public power. They did not want any permanent physical attachments to their homesteads that would cause dependence on the outside world: no telephone wires, no electrical wires, and no water or gas lines. They live "off the grid," so to speak.

But that doesn't mean they live without power. They are remarkably energy efficient, but they don't rely on one energy source as the English do—they use a combination of sources. In fact, as energy prices squeeze families' budgets, energy experts might find themselves heralding the efficiency of the Amish.

Alva and Menno use a windmill and gravity to provide running water to their house. The next farm over uses a waterwheel. Alva's refrigerator has a hum to it—the sound comes from the propane gas tube that snakes behind it to feed it. She uses kerosene to heat the water she needs. LED headlamps are by the back door for morning and evening trips to the barn.

Out in the dairy barn, a large rumbling noise starts up. The pelting rain can't drown out that noise—it's like standing inside a jet engine. Alva said the sound belonged to Menno's diesel generator, cranking to life. He used it to provide electricity to run his milking machines. She said the generator was much less expensive than if Menno used public utility power. The Amish have perfected the use of small fuel-efficient motors to run machinery or modern power tools: generators, air compressors, and diesel engines. Some Amish businesses use word processors run on generators.

Most Amish will say they do not want electricity in their homes because they want to keep out the influence on their children of television, computers, and video games. They aren't against using power tools, like gas-powered weed whackers, because they are not seen as a threat to their lifestyle and families. And that priority is really at the heart of eschewing dependence on public utilities: avoiding it is a way to insulate their homes.

Outside, lightning started to sizzle against the darkened skies. Unconcerned, Alva set up the ironing board and hunted for a match. The little iron she lit was a lightweight Coleman gas model with instant blue flames. Once hot, she started to tackle that big basket of clean laundry.

Another bonus to self-sufficient energy: the Amish do not worry about power outages.

REFLECTIONS ON SIMPLICITY

How dependent are you on modern conveniences? Which ones are needs and which ones are luxuries?

Sometimes, we get our wants and our needs mixed up. Think about ways to be less dependent on energy. How can that help you live simply?

Have you ever tried to scale back your nonessential expenditures for a period of time, such as not going out to eat in restaurants? What was the result? Did you find that it made you appreciate going out more? Or did you discover that you didn't miss it?

The Amish believe less is more. How does that help them live a simpler, less complicated life?

PLAIN *Living*

In 1955, Jay Lehman was concerned that some day the Amish would not be able to maintain their simple ways because their non-electric products would no longer be available. He founded a store in Kidron, Ohio; today, that store is the world's largest provider of historical technology. His goal was, and still is, to provide authentic, historical products to those seeking a simpler life: Homesteaders, environmentalists, missionaries, doctors in developing nations, and others living in areas where there is no power or unreliable power rely on Lehman's. Hollywood set designers too. Lehman has supplied historically accurate period pieces for many movies.[10]

Part 2

Time

Live each short hour with God and the long years will take care of themselves.

Amish Proverb

There's more traffic on Route 30 in Pennsylvania than there used to be. But turn off the highway east of Bird-in-Hand, drive down the two-lane road, past the stream flanked by cattails that runs under the road, and stop when you reach the gravel lane of a big white farmhouse. Suddenly, Route 30 belongs to another world.

The farmhouse belongs to Jonas and Mary Glick, dairy farmers who were kind enough to let me spend a day with them to learn all that I could about, well, bovines. Before I went, I knew one thing: the dairy cow is the backbone of the family farm. But that's about all I knew.

On the day of my visit, Mary greets me at my car with a delighted look on her face. "You're just in time!" she says eagerly. "A cow has just 'freshed'!"

Freshed? Before I can open my mouth to ask, Mary has spun on her bare feet and is on her way to the milking barn. Mary is a sturdy, Germanic-looking woman, as round as she is tall. Her legs remind me of pistons in a car, pumping rhythmically as she runs from barn to house to car and back again.

As soon as Mary disappears into the barn, a willowy girl, slender as a pump handle, appears by my side. "I'm Sara," she says, staring at me with unmasked curiosity. "Mom's gone to see the freshed cow."

"What does that mean?" I ask her.

Sara tries, unsuccessfully, to suppress a grin at my ignorance. "It means she just delivered a calf."

I trot behind Sara to go meet this fresh cow. The dark, cool barn is a sour mélange of earthy smells: fresh hay, musty animals, and manure. As my eyes adjust to the dim light, I see Jonas and Mary standing by a stall, a look of awe on their faces as if witnessing a miracle. I quietly walk over to see what captures their attention. It's a baby calf struggling to stand on her wobbly legs for the first time.

Jonas, whose ginger beard lies on his chest like a forkful of hay, acknowledges my presence with a quick nod. His gaze returns to the mother cow, now licking her baby's face. He lets out a deeply satisfied sigh. "I never get tired of that."

Then the miracle passes and it's time to get back to business. Jonas turns to me and says, "Well, you said you wanted to learn about the dairy. So, come on then."

I spend the next few hours shadowing Jonas, trying to keep out of his way, asking so many questions I worry I'm annoying him, scribbling down notes so I won't forget. When Jonas finally sits down to untangle some baling twine, I ask him about his childhood. "Oh, it was a wonderful experience," Jonas says of growing up on a dairy farm.

"What about now?" I ask. Even I can see the endless demands. "You're pretty tied to the clock with dairy cows. And such early hours!" He told me he is out of bed, milking cows, at 4 a.m. every day. And milking them again at 4 p.m. There's no such thing as a day off for a dairy farmer. Even on Sunday, the ever-faithful cows need to be milked.

"I love my dairy. Love my farm too." Elbows straight, his hands rest on his knees. "My father taught us that the farm was more than just our home. It's a responsibility. It's a little slice of paradise. It's meant to be passed on to others."

He springs to his feet and tosses the now untangled twine on his workbench. "And that's just what happened," he tells me in what I would call a voice of quiet pride. Jonas's farm has been in the family for four generations, and he is hoping it will continue on with one of his sons. When Jonas talks about the passing of time, it sounds sweet and unending, like a gently flowing river.

As many chores as Jonas has, I notice that he often stops to observe something in nature that fills him with wonder, like the birth of the calf or the song of the vesper sparrow or the lifting of a tiger swallowtail butterfly into the sky. Time might pass slowly on Amish farms, but it is filled with promise about what is to come: small miracles in the course of a day, long miracles of passing generations.

By late afternoon I have learned so much about dairy cows, I think I am ready to go. Jonas says no. I have to feed the new calves. My brain is nearly saturated with bovine knowledge, but I smile and follow him out to where the calves are housed in their little plastic igloos. He hands me a gigantic baby bottle filled with milk and points to a calf named Teacup. She lunges for me and latches on to the bottle as if it is her last meal.

Unbefitting to her name, Teacup is not a dainty eater. She's a slob. Thankfully, she has no upper teeth to bite, but her sandpaper tongue is rough and powerfully strong. She slurps and drools and splatters me with warm milk. But I don't mind. I'm not quite so eager to get back on the highway and join the traffic jam. In fact, I'm reconsidering Mary's offer to stay for dinner, even though it will mean I need to help wash dinner dishes. A lot of them.

Three hours and 281 dishes later, I leave Jonas and Mary's farm feeling deeply satisfied and deeply tired. Life is hard work: that is one lesson a farm teaches. Life is filled with beauty and wonder and hope for tomorrow: that is another.

Sue Bender on Time

Enjoy today, it won't come back.

Amish Proverb

In 1967, artist and family therapist Sue Bender felt a tug-of-war raging inside her. One summer, she found herself drawn to Amish quilts displayed in a clothing store and became completely enamored. That summer, each time she went back to gaze at them—those stoic Amish quilts with their Spartan shapes—she felt shock waves running through her. "I had an obsession with the Amish," Sue admits. "I, who worked hard at being special, fell in love with a people who valued being ordinary."

Dissatisfied with the frantic pace she had been living, she was desperate to find a way to live a more intentional, less frazzled life. She could not ignore the inexplicable calling she felt to go to the Amish. She took out an advertisement in *The Budget*, asking if an Amish family would allow her to come and stay with them for a while. Six months later, one Amish woman responded to Sue, inviting her for a visit. Sue grabbed the opportunity. She soaked up the experience, finding that it fed her soul. A year later, she stayed with another Amish family. She spent months with each family, entering a world without television, telephones, or electricity. Eventually, she made seven such visits. Profoundly touched, Bender wrote of her sojourn in *Plain and Simple: A Woman's Journey to the Amish.*

The use of time among the Amish captivated Sue. To her, time was a burden. "There was never enough of it," she felt. She noticed that the Amish valued the process as well as the finished product. The women she lived with moved through the day unhurried. There was no rushing to finish so they could get on to the "important things." For them, Sue observed, it was all important. There was no distinction between the sacred and the ordinary. To Sue, such a concept was astounding.

> In Berkeley I ran around breathlessly rushing toward impossible goals—and to that vague "something out there." When I explained how split I was, loving to do certain things and hating to do others, the women laughed and tried to understand.
>
> "Making a batch of vegetable soup, it's not right for the carrot to say I taste better than the peas, or the pea to say I taste better than the cabbage. It takes all the vegetables to make a good soup!" Miriam said.[1]

Twenty years after *Plain and Simple*'s publication, Sue is just as committed to practicing those principles she gleaned while living with the Amish. "It's much harder than I thought it would be," she admitted. "I knew I could never be Amish, but I still have the same conclusions. Nothing different has come to me. It's the same principles: honoring the ordinary things, to be fully present in the moment, to have an overriding sense of purpose. It's not mysterious. I just try to take those principles in everyday life: How do I treat the barista who makes my cappuccino? How do I not take small things for granted?"

Generally, when someone agrees to be interviewed, it is good policy to allow her to see the finished copy for approval. For corrections too. Sue waived that offer away, as if shooing the butler.

"I trust you," she said. "That's another thing I've learned from the Amish. To trust."

REFLECTIONS ON TIME

Although much time is saved with our modern conveniences, for some reason there is less of it. Is that true for you? If so, why do you think that is?

For a lot of people, slowing down means getting their hands on something: they write letters in longhand even though they have computers, or hand wash dishes though they have dishwashers. Do you enjoy doing manual tasks? Is there one in particular that helps slow you down?

For some people, slowing down means taking moments of stillness: spending a sunny afternoon gardening with a daughter; reading a good book by the fireplace on a rainy day; taking the dog for a walk in the early morning, when the world is just waking up. What reminders do you have to stop and let your mind be still and open?

In a high-tech, fast-paced world, we are continually bombarded with information, opportunities, and demands. People have little time to reflect and often lose track of what is really important. How does slowing down create more room in your life to wait on God?

PLAIN *Living*

Some Amish participate in what are known as circle letters, whereby a group is formed and each person adds a letter to a pack of letters that goes around and around a circle of about a dozen people, each adding his own and sending it on. Circle letters are popular among different groups—spread-out family members, groups of teachers, wheelchair-bound individuals, organic farmers, and Amish bishops, among others. There is also the Ohio-to-Ontario "Andy Mast Circle Letter"— consisting of fourteen Amish with the same name.[2]

The Clockless Year

Days are like suitcases, all the same size, but some people are able to pack more into them than others.

Amish Proverb

I t is late in the day on a Saturday. The moon is rising over freshly plowed fields, competing with the last glimmer of light from the sun as the day gives way its light. An enormous white farmhouse sits on a piece of property that is as picturesque as a postcard. A majestic willow tree—with a fort tucked in its limbs and a wooden swing hanging off of a branch—is nestled next to a creek. Ewes and their small white lambs baa and bleat as they graze in the tender green grass. Even the name of the farm seems pastoral: Weeping Willow Farm.

Ah, *such* a peaceful picture.

But look again.

There is a beehive of activity going on at this farm. Marvin and Rachel Yoder, the owners of the farm, and their eight children, ages twelve to twenty-eight, are adding a "spit and polish" to their property. Two girls are putting fresh mulch on the roses and the tulip bed. One holds a flashlight with one hand, a bag of mulch open with the other. Her sister spreads the mulch with a shovel and carefully tamps it around the base of the flowers. Two other girls are weed whacking the edges of the freshly mown lawn. The boys are sweeping out the barn and the driveway. Rachel is in the house cooking. In the air is a buzz of anticipation, almost palpable.

Come Monday morning, 160 ministers will gather at Weeping Willow Farm for a meeting, an annual event that rotates among ministers' farms. The Yoders are doing everything they can to ready their home for this important day. Tomorrow is Sunday, so all preparations must be finished by tonight.

It's obvious that the ministers' meeting is a very significant occurrence. The Yoders have closed down their guest house for the weekend—a small cabin converted into a bed-and-breakfast business, revenue they count on. "A lot of ladies come here for getaways," Marvin says. "Last week we had five sisters come to stay. The week before, it was five women friends." To accommodate their technology-enmeshed visitors, Marvin invented a solar battery pack for cabin use. It's a solar panel, plus a battery, plus an inverter that is portable and capable of running fans. Not air conditioning, though.

"If you look through the guest book," Rachel says, pointing to a large book on the table, "you'll see that we have folks from Australia, Japan, China, and Europe." She sounds surprised that people would travel such a distance to visit an ordinary Amish dairy farm.

On the other hand, Rachel has no desire to be anywhere *but* here. Her roots run deep in these seventy acres, as deep as the willow tree her father had planted along the creek, many years ago. This is the only home she has ever known. An only child, she was born in the farmhouse. Her father, like her husband, is a minister. When Rachel married Marvin, he took over managing Weeping Willow's dairy, and her parents moved into the Grossdaadi Haus. This is the first time Weeping Willow will host the ministers' meeting.

The next time it occurs, the farm will belong to one of her future grandsons or great-grandsons, but only if he is chosen by lot to become a minister like his relatives once were.

This farm holds a continuity of life to Rachel. Generations overlap here, creating a passing of time that is slow and sweet and rich with meaning. Her life is governed by the same yearly cycle that arranged her mother's life. The four seasons order the flow of Rachel's daily work in her household and her farm. She doesn't even bother to wear a wristwatch. In fact, the Amish keep their own time—they don't conform to Daylight Savings. Their clock is the sun. Their calendar is the earth as it turns on its axis, dividing a year into seasons.

Late spring and early summer are Rachel's time for tending gardens and yards. In the front of her farmhouse for all to see is an artfully designed flower garden—the one her daughters are mulching. Directly behind the house is a substantial vegetable garden, bigger than most people's backyards. When the garden's produce begins to ripen, canning and preserving are done, continuing until the first frost. Canning and preserving food is the major work of Rachel's summer, requiring much time and effort. Most families put up more than 800 quarts of fruit, vegetables, and meat every summer to last them for the year.

In the late fall, Rachel does a major housecleaning, preparing the house and gardens for the winter months. The winter months are the slowest time, she says, since there is little farmwork other than the constant care of their herd of dairy cows. Those are the months in which Rachel sews and quilts. She and her daughters sew nearly all of the clothes the family wears. November and December is also wedding season: most Amish weddings take place after the harvest is finished and the land is resting.

As soon as the ground is ready to work in the early spring, Rachel starts her garden. Two cold frames help her get the jump on lettuce and garden seedlings. Spring also means another major housecleaning. This year, Rachel is able to combine the housecleaning with preparations for the ministers' meeting.

It is now early Monday morning. Dozens of Amish buggies are lined up shoulder to shoulder in the Yoders' long gravel driveway, behind the barn, and along the fences. The ministers' horses are fed and stabled by Rachel and Marvin's sons. Rachel and her daughters run back and forth between the barn and the kitchen, putting last-minute touches on the lunch. The ministers are gathered in the barn to share a time of worship, discuss concerns, and prepare to care for their flock for another year.

Everything and everyone meaningful to Rachel is right here, at Weeping Willow Farm. Her past, her future, her family, her supportive and extended community.

Why would she want to go anywhere else?

REFLECTIONS ON TIME

Rachel's home has great meaning to her; it holds her history and those whom she loves. What home has been most meaningful to you?

Do you appreciate your familial history? Some people research their family's genealogy and create memoirs from old letters and diaries. Other families plan annual reunions. What can you do to strengthen your bond with your extended family?

What elements of continuity are in your life? An heirloom handed down, a tradition? How can you celebrate those legacies of your heritage?

How conscious are you of the passing of time? How does it make you feel? What steps can you take to cherish the time God has given to you?

PLAIN *Living*

Mounting evidence indicates that the Amish maintain one of the strongest and most stable family systems in America. This is due, in part, to the peaceable, slow-paced, stress-free lifestyle they live. Research indicates that living within a culture that provides such a well-defined social identity and support system is of great value to its participants, both psychologically and physically. For example, researchers have provided data indicating that major depression occurs about one-fifth to one-tenth as often among Old Order Amish individuals as it does among the rest of the United States population. In addition, the Harvard School of Medicine's recent findings revealed that Amish people have a much lower rate of heart disease than do average Americans.[3]

The Team

More is caught than taught.

Amish Proverb

On a sunny autumn afternoon, fourteen-year-old Levi Mast and his father are on their way home from a horse auction run by Alvin Gingerich, a man known by the handle of Auction Al. Behind their buggy is tied a young Standardbred gelding, Silver.

Every few minutes, Levi cranes his neck to look through the back window of the buggy to see how Silver is coping with the traffic. Stopped at a red light, Levi smiles to see Silver swishing his tail at a pesky fly. A beauty with slender, graceful lines and near perfect conformation, Silver will be Levi's responsibility to train. He isn't buggy broke yet, so it will be up to Levi to teach him to grow accustomed to the harness traces and to become reliable in traffic. Levi feels pleased that his father has confidence in him to train a horse. His father had even let him bid on Silver at Auction Al's.

Levi wants to become a horse breeder one day. Just last week, his father had spoken to Eli Yoder, the smithy, about fielding Levi out as an apprentice after he finishes school this spring. Levi won't get paid, and he knows his friends will tease him and call him a horse pedicurist, but he doesn't mind. Nothing can ever change how he feels about horses. He loves horses. Always has, as far back as he can remember.

Levi has a plan to save up money to buy a registered Standardbred mare for the purpose of starting a small herd. When he told his father about his idea, he was surprised that his father was agreeable to it. Not just agreeable—he said he'd chip in. His father said that the demand for registered Standardbreds to pull fast-moving Amish buggies would make the venture profitable. "One thing you can count on," his father told him, "Plain People will always have need for a good buggy horse."

The Amish use Standardbred horses to pull their buggies—usually race horses that didn't quite cut it at the track or had been retired. There are a couple of reasons: the Standardbred is the world's fastest horse under harness, and unlike the Thoroughbred, its origins are entirely American. All registered Standardbred horses can trace their lineage back to Justin Morgan, the stallion owned by a New England schoolteacher from which the breed descends.

The horse, to the Amish, is not just another farm animal. Fondly called "the team" by the family, the horse and buggy symbolize much more than transportation—they're central to the Amish way of life. Dependence on the horse restricts the distance one can travel—keeping families close to home—and it also restricts the pace—constraining a to-do list. The gait of the horse is gentle and steady, calmly lulling the senses. The scenery doesn't whiz by in a buggy, it unrolls. There is time enough to notice the color of changing leaves on trees, or the horses grazing in a pasture, or the height of the corn in a farmer's field.

In the early 1900s, as automobiles started to appear on the American horizon, Amish bishops debated the potential impact of the automobile on their way of life. With sentient foresight, they worried people in "horseless carriages" would spread out in opposite directions and no longer need a tight-knit community.

The bishops chose to forbid car ownership for church members, preferring the horse and buggy with its leisurely pace of five to ten miles per hour. Such an imposed limitation, they felt, would create natural boundaries and increase reliance on the community.

Today, the horse and buggy are a cherished and recognizable symbol of Amish identity. Their black silhouette is as recognizable as McDonald's golden arches or the Nike swoosh. See a buggy and a horse on a road sign or a billboard and, instantly, the message is clear: Slow down! You've entered another world.

REFLECTIONS ON TIME

Before accepting or buying a new technology, have you ever thought, what will come next? What will this lead to? How will this change how I use time?

In what specific ways has technology—those electronic gizmos designed to save us more time—ended up stealing your time? Does technology sometimes delude you into thinking you're saving time when just the opposite is happening? If so, how can you change that?

What obstacles have you found to slowing down? How might these be eliminated or better managed?

What kind of imposed limitations are in your life? What kinds of benefits do they provide?

PLAIN *Living*

There may be several buggies [in an Amish household] for everyday use, depending on how many children in the family are old enough to drive. A large family might own a two-seat buggy, which is the Amish version of the station wagon. Naturally, no self-respecting young man would dream of borrowing the stodgy two-seater to take to the Sunday evening social.[4]

The Patient Farmer

To mistreat God's creation is to offend the Creator.

Amish Proverb

On a Monday morning, if you ask a farmer what he plans to do for the week, he'll look at you as if you're crazy," says David Kline, an Old Order Amish bishop in central Ohio. "He knows that it all depends on the weather." He laughs. "I like that about farming. God makes us aware of our limitations through weather."

David grew up on the 120-acre farm in north-central Ohio where he now lives with his wife, along with forty-five Jersey cows and two bulls, Junior and Mike. David's five children are grown now with farms of their own; he has seventeen grandchildren and counting.

Of the Klines' 120 rolling acres, seventy are tillable. They have two permanent gardens; they grow feed for their livestock as well as their own vegetables, potatoes, and grass-fed beef. The rest of the land is made up of woodland, orchards, barns, and an unofficial refuge for all wildlife. Migratory birds are invited to share the Klines' land too and are encouraged to visit and stay for a while. "Nothing is harmed on this property. We work with nature. Even the dung beetles serve a purpose, putting everything back in sync."

The Amish have always been people of the land. In Europe, they had an ability to transform unproductive lands into fertile farms. They excelled as farmers in Switzerland, Alsace, and Germany. As early as the seventeenth century, they practiced indoor feeding of livestock, rotation of crops, and meadow irrigation; they used animal fertilizer; and they raised new varieties of clover as a means of restoring soil fertility. David says that Amish farming is really traditional farming. They plow with horses to avoid compacting the soil. "It takes five years of horse plowing and natural manure to get the soil to the point where I like it."

Innovations and improvements have been added along the way. "The Amish are not necessarily anti-technologists," David says. "We have simply chosen not to be controlled by technology."

When no-till farming with its dependence on chemicals was the craze, David knew that the promised green fields would also be strangely silent. "Small-scale diversified farming actually enhances wildlife." He does not use insecticides. "We don't need them." The cycles of crop rotation, pasturing the fields, adding manure, then top-seeding with nitrogen-laden legume seeds all contribute to keep the soil healthy. "There are no crop-damaging insects, except Japanese beetles in the yard." If there are some weeds and grasses in the corn, David says that it actually benefits the topsoil. In summer in Ohio, thundershowers can dump several inches of rain in a brief span of time, more than even the most absorbent soil can take. Weeds hold the topsoil in place.

David repays his animals for the work they do for him by kindness. "We provide the best possible life for them that they could desire. Even the wildlife is treated with kindness." On the Klines' farm, hay-cutting is delayed to let the young ground-nesting birds finish raising their fledglings.

Work on an Amish farm is spread out from spring to fall, beginning with plowing the sod in March. "This is our 'quiet time,'" David explains. "A time to listen to God and his creation as we are a part of the unfolding of spring." April and May are the planting months. "By June, the bird migration is over and summer settles in, and so do the birds." An avid bird-watcher, David and his family did a survey of nesting birds around their farm buildings. Within 200 feet of their house, they counted 13 species and over 1800 young fledglings, which, of course, included the 300-nest cliff swallow colony.

"Life and work on the farm peaks in July," he says. "August hints of autumn and silo filling, early applesauce, and the call of insects." On rainy days, David writes or fishes. In October, after the corn is harvested, the silos are filled with the help of neighbors. The fieldwork comes to a close.

By living close to nature, the Amish believe they stay in touch with God. They feel that the rhythms of nature, the changing seasons, and the struggle with weather all provide opportunities to experience divine presence.

"The year is a never-ending adventure," David says. His smile is one of pure satisfaction and contentment.

REFLECTIONS ON TIME

The Amish revere nature as part of God's divine creation. "The heavens declare the glory of God; the skies proclaim the work of his hands. Day after day they pour forth speech; night after night they display knowledge" (Ps. 19:1–2). How does nature inspire you to worship God?

In what ways does technology control your day? How can you choose not to be controlled by it?

"We need time," David says, "to savor the special things in life: to take a child's hand in our own and share in the child's wonder at the unfolding of a leaf, the blue of a robin's egg, a bee on the yellow blossom of coltsfoot." Identify a time in your life when you slowed down and enjoyed an experience that came your way.

What helped lead you to this time of slowing? How did it benefit you? Today, take a moment to savor a special thing in your life. Ask God to teach you the discipline of slowing down.

PLAIN *Living*

The fertility of the soil, the many sources of water, and the cheapness of land in Lancaster County are what initially attracted the Amish to the New World, along with William Penn's offer to take part in the "holy experiment" of an area devoted to religious freedom. Land-poor in Europe, the Amish leaped at the chance to own good land.[5]

Going In with the Boys

God likes small people. He cannot use big ones.

Amish Proverb

Back in the summer of 1951, Sam Stoltzfus was eight years old. The world was big and wondrous, and there was a significant event coming up in his small boy's world. He would soon be going in with the boys into the Amish church service. This usually happened when an Amish boy turned nine.

In Sam's church, there were closely followed routines for the congregation to enter the house or barn where the church service was held. At 8 a.m., the ministers would walk in by order of their being ordained. Next, the married men would file in by age, oldest to youngest. Next, the women and girls. The men sat on one side, the women on the other.

At twenty minutes after eight, someone would come and tell the boys to get ready to go in. "They would brush off their trousers and the big boys would comb their hair," Sam said. Ten minutes later, the boys would walk in, shake the ministers' hands, and sit down just behind them on three or four long benches. "Going in with the boys was a big ritual in our Amish world—the first rite of passage from boyhood to being big. The next step would be when a boy turned sixteen and got a horse and buggy and began 'running around.' Next to first day of school, going in with the boys was a big milestone. Every Sunday morning we'd watch the older boys with envy. They looked so big and important coming into the meeting room."

But there was one task Sam had to do before he could go in with the boys. His mother insisted that he memorize the *Lob Lied* (Hymn of Praise). The *Lob Lied* is a twenty-eight-line hymn, all in high German, sung as the second hymn at Amish church services. "This looked like a big task for an eight-year-old with lots of other things to read," Sam said. "But I wanted to go in with the boys so badly that I worked hard on it that summer. I had already learned several small children's prayers and had memorized the Lord's Prayer. Mom had given me a little present then. But the *Lob Lied* was much harder."

All through the month of August, Sam worked hard to learn the *Lob Lied*. "I recall saying it over and over and often stumbling over the words. Mom would praise me when I got it right, but she would frown if I missed a word. It didn't matter how hard I tried. I didn't know it all by my ninth birthday, and Mom said I could not go in with the boys."

The next church Sunday, Sam felt awkward because all the church boys knew it was his birthday. He knew they were wondering why he didn't go in with the boys. "Mom didn't allow any shortcuts."

So it was back to studying more and reciting more until Sam could finally repeat the entire twenty-eight lines without missing a syllable. His mother smiled and told him, "Now you may go in with the boys."

That first Sunday morning will be forever etched in Sam's memory. "We boys liked to watch the big boys come with their horses and buggies. Cousin Hans always saw who had the fastest horse and the fanciest harness. Finally, the farm's owner came and called us to go in. We'd all use the restroom—a nearby horse stall or barn corner—and then we'd be ready."

His mother had cued him how to enter the room. "Mom had told me again and again, 'Just shake hands with the ministers, the ones with their hats on, not the older men.'" Sam remembered how he felt walking in that first time with his friends. "I can also remember well shaking hands with the four ministers, who looked so reverent with their hats on. Amos U. was first—he looked so wise. Then came Ephraim, always with a smile, followed by Uncle Sylvan's kindly face. Deacon Aaron was last and had such nice twinkly eyes."

Then Sam would sit on a bench next to his cousins, sharing the *Ausbund* hymnbook. "When the *Lob Lied* was sung, I could read the lines and help sing. All forenoon we had to sit still and listen to the preacher. Mom had warned me that if I didn't behave, I'd have to sit with her." He tried, without success, to keep a grin from spreading across his face. "That happened once or so."

REFLECTIONS ON TIME

What kind of rituals were part of your childhood? Looking back, did they have meaning to you? Do they now? If so, what changed?

If you don't know why you're keeping rules or observing rituals, they can seem meaningless. Why do you think Sam felt so committed to memorizing the hymn? What did it do for him, besides giving him the nod to sit with the boys?

Going to church on Sunday is highly valued in the Amish culture. They prepare for it on Saturday afternoon and arrive early for it. What are some ways your family could value church more?

PLAIN *Living*

The Amish speak three distinctive tongues. [Their first language is] Pennsylvania German, called Dutch, though it has no connection to the Netherlands. The second language of the growing Amish child is English. Amish children learn to speak the two languages without difficulty and without noticeable accent. Upon entering school the child frequently has only a very limited grasp of English, but readily learns English as a second language. [The third language is] a passive knowledge of High German, used primarily when the Bible is read aloud or quoted.[6]

Experience Is the Great Teacher

Beware of the man who knows the answer before he understands the question.

Amish Proverb

In 1965, David Kline was drafted into the Vietnam War. He served two years working in a hospital in Cleveland, Ohio, as a conscientious objector. When he left his parents' Amish farm for the city, he knew he might not return. He felt he was gravitating toward a different life. "I was struggling," he admitted. "I just loved to learn." His voice nearly broke on the word "learn," as if it were sacred.

But when his service ended, David chose to return to his Old Order Amish roots. He didn't realize what community was until he left it. "It's like an old coat. You aren't aware of it until it's taken away." It's not that he didn't chafe against the restrictions on technology and higher education. He did. He still does. He's a highly intelligent man who has authored two books of natural essays and started a magazine for small farms. He returned to a community that, he said, chose to work with their hands, believing manual labor was close to godliness.

Returning to the fold didn't squelch David's intellectual curiosity, nor has it denied him an active mental life. If anything, his time of duty in Cleveland gave him a heightened appreciation for the informal style of Amish education. It's one based on learning by seeing and doing what adults are doing—the epitome of experiential learning. Skills are learned by observation, trial and error, and repetition. "In this culture," he said, "you learn from a master. There is always someone who possesses the arts and skills one needs."

Back on the farm, David discovered that his network of extended family and fellow Amish provided a rich educational environment. His role models weren't entertainment celebrities or athletes but local people and neighbors. People like his uncle, who lived on the next farm and read voraciously. Or another neighbor, gifted with horses, who taught David about handling and loving the gentle draft horse. Later, that neighbor lost his larynx to cancer. "But his horses responded to his slightest touch of the lines," David remembered. "Mel taught me so much about horses."

Farm life provides ample opportunities for children to work side by side with adults. During threshing time, they help in the field to stack the sheaves of grain on the wagons. "Here the art of correctly loading the bundles—heads inward, knots down, butts out a bit from the wagon edge, the center filled but not too full, watch out for thistles—is taught by older brothers or sisters, fathers or neighbors," David said.

At a barn raising or a quilting bee, children shadow older siblings or adults and are given small tasks to complete. Little boys practice hammering with stray nails they've collected on the ground. Little girls practice small, even stitches by sewing quilt pieces together. With adolescence and the completion of eighth grade come more regular jobs, a type of apprenticeship.

Something else happens when a child works side by side with his parent. "I don't know what it is about the muckery, but it's when we're mucking out our horse stables that my son and I have our best discussions," said David. "It's here where I think I see subtle signs that he shares his parents' view that 'a man is rich in proportion to the things he can afford to leave alone.' As I reach out and put my hand on his shoulder, I say, 'Son, if at times you forget the admonishing I've done and advice I've given over the years, don't forget the good talks we've had in this stable. But above all else, please remember that your mother and I love you very much.'" David shrugged. "It was the same way with my dad. We had long talks as we mucked out stables. There is something about that strenuous work—maybe it's the aroma—that melts away communication barriers."

The English would call it "bonding."

REFLECTIONS ON TIME

We often call our work "making a living." What is implied in that?

Is it possible to be grateful you have work to do but not see much significance in that job? If that's how you feel, do you think something needs to change so that you find more meaning in your work?

Passing on skills to a child takes time but offers lifelong rewards. Cooking together, carpentry, gardening, playing a sport. What talents or skills did your parents give to you? Which ones can you pass on to your children?

PLAIN *Living*

Pennsylvania German, primarily an oral language, is the familiar tongue of children at home and in informal conversations. It is the mother tongue of children born to Amish parents. This is a distinct dialect of the German language. The dialect resembles the Palatine German folk speech. It is spoken by people of other religious denominations, including Lutheran, Reformed, and Church of the Brethren, who also originated in German-speaking areas.[7]

A Margin of Error

A task takes as long as it takes.

Amish Proverb

Elizabeth, a young woman in her late teens, has three older sisters and five older brothers. "As I was growing up," she said, "I remember wanting to do the things my sisters did. When I was three years old, we had a quilting bee to quilt one of my sister's quilts. I got the idea in my head that I'd like to try quilting too. So I asked Mom for a needle and thread and put in a few stitches. I didn't think those first few stitches looked very good. They were uneven, so I pulled them all out. What I found out was that quilting takes time and practice and that after time I got better."

Imitating older sisters is the chief objective of most every little girl, Amish or not, but there the similarity ends. Elizabeth's awareness that her stitches were uneven, her determination to pull them out and try again, and the patience to not get frustrated and give up . . . at the age of three! Well, it boggles the mind.

The work ethic of the Amish had already been instilled in Elizabeth, even at her tender age. The Amish are known for their precise craftsmanship, be it quilting, carpentry, cooking, or blacksmithing. Doing something well is a virtue. Even in school, children learn a concept thoroughly before moving on to the next assignment. They value thoroughness over haste, completion over speed. To the Amish way of thinking, a task takes the time that it takes. They also value giving a task the time it requires to do a job well. Elizabeth didn't feel frustrated or impatient with herself, as so many do—including adults—while on the steep learning curve.

So how do the Amish instill such a work ethic in their children?

It's not as complicated as it sounds. In fact, it's something we all do, whether we intend to or not. It's called *modeling*.

Elizabeth's community is made up of living examples—good ones—of how to work, how to live, and how to love others. She is surrounded by a covey of females: mothers, grandmothers, sisters, and cousins who pass on their knowledge and expertise about how to cook, clean, quilt, and be keepers of the home—all of the components that make up an Amish woman's life—as naturally as sharing the air they breathe.

These women know what they're doing. There's always a skilled grandmother nearby to help out. Elizabeth has grown up watching these women take care in each step, in everything they do, observing that doing something well takes time. The slow, unhurried pace of the Plain People allows for a margin of error, so necessary in the learning curve. Their life is not packed with an endless to-do list. They are busy, productive people, but their day permits room to breathe.

Elizabeth enjoyed sewing so much that she used to gather scraps of fabric together, left over from quilting bees. "I used them to make doll quilts before I was old enough to go to school and could hardly reach the treadle." By the age of twelve, her quilting skills had become so precise that her tiny stitches almost seemed to disappear. She was working on her first quilt, a Log Cabin pattern, when a customer came into her mother's quilt shop and told her he wanted to buy it. "That really got me sewing!" she said. Now eighteen, she still enjoys sewing.

The Plain have a saying, "Pride in your work puts joy in your day." One of the benefits of attention to detail is the pleasure one can take in one's work, that deep-down satisfaction in a job done well. That's the way work should be.

REFLECTIONS ON TIME

One Amish man joked that if he were meant to plow at night, God would have put a headlight on a horse. The Amish respect natural limitations: sunlight and seasons, hunger and fatigue. Do you accept those limitations, or do you try to override them? Do you ever feel as if you are expecting too much from yourself?

How many times in a day do you feel rushed? How many times in a day do you feel frustrated? Are those moments always related to each other? Building a margin of error into your schedule—for unexpected things like traffic jams—can be a simple and effective way to add peace to your life.

The Amish have extra time in their day because they have eliminated television, daily newspapers, computers. If you're struggling for time, drowning in your to-do list, try one week of cutting back on time wasters. See if your time expands.

PLAIN *Living*

Rumspringa means "running around." When Amish youth turn sixteen, they begin to go out with their peers on weekends and are given some leeway by their parents. It is perceived as a time to explore the outside world and count the cost of membership before joining the church. "The Amish count on the Rumspringa process to inoculate youth against the strong pull of the forbidden by dosing them with the vaccine of a little worldly experience. Their gamble is also based on the notion that there is no firmer adhesive bond to a faith and way of life than a bond freely chosen, in this case chosen after Rumspringa and having sampled some of the available alternative ways of living."[8]

Growing Old Amish

Our duty is not to see through one another but to see one another through.

Amish Proverb

Julia Schlabach never expected her father to die at an early age. Only sixty-three, he was fit and active, much more so than her mother. "After Dad died, we all wanted Mom to come live with us," Julia said, "but she decided to sell the farm to my youngest brother and live in the small house down the lane from the main farmhouse." Julia has nine brothers and sisters; all but one brother have joined the Amish church. "We all try and look after Mom. She had been doing okay, but we could tell that she needed some help around the house."

Last Christmas, Julia's sister handed everyone a list of dates. "My sister Mary Sue thought it up. She assigned everyone to take a turn and help Mom for one day per week throughout the year," Julia explained. "We mow her lawns or do her laundry; whatever she needs. I thought it was a real good idea, and it's worked out well."

The grandchildren participate too by running errands or hoeing the garden. "Everyone plays a part," Julia said. "I like having my children see how to take good care of a grandmother. She's taken good care of all of us over the years. She's been a wonderful mother and grandmother. It's our turn, now, to take care of her."

The Amish view time passing in their own lives as a benefit. The older you get, the wiser you become. The elderly among them are considered sage givers on nearly every topic: health and illness, household chores and cooking, gardening, farming, even predicting the weather. Julia said that a main theme of Amish preaching is the commandment "Honour thy father and thy mother: that thy days may be long upon the land which the LORD thy God giveth thee" (Exod. 20:12 KJV).

After Julia and Tom were married, Tom's parents decided it was time to move into the Grossdaadi Haus. Tom was ready to take over the farm, but his father, John D., still stayed involved. "John D. wasn't quite as ready to move off the farm as my mother-in-law was. I think John D. wanted to make sure Tom wouldn't run the farm into the ground," Julia said with a grin. "John D. likes to have an influence." John D. and his wife, Lorena, shop and prepare their own meals, as well as have their own horse and buggy. Still, they're just a shout away.

Lately, that proximity has been more than a comfort. John D. suffers from emphysema and asthma. During the last winter, he became very ill with pneumonia. "We thought for sure he was going to pass," Julia said. All of John D.'s grown children took turns by his bedside. Tom stayed each night in the Grossdaadi Haus and slept in a cot near his father's bed, just in case his father needed help in the night. John D. rallied and recovered, but he is quite frail. An oxygen tank is never far.

Relatives care for their elderly, despite inconvenience or hardship, even for a disease as difficult as Alzheimer's. Julia said that one family in her church district had a great-grandfather with Alzheimer's disease. "It was hard. This fellow would get up in the night and wander outside. Seven years! He's passed on now, but the family took great comfort in knowing they were able to care for him in the very home he had been born in. They knew that was what God wanted." Julia said that every member of the extended family took a shift, around the clock, to care for the great-grandfather. Even the teenagers. Responsibility ebbs and flows between generations.

To grow old Amish means growing old with dignity, not despair. Appreciation, not anxiety. Surrounded by loving family members, not loneliness. No, never loneliness.

REFLECTIONS ON TIME

The Amish seem to face old age with grace and acceptance. Would you find it difficult to "retire" and move to a Grossdaadi Haus? (We might call it *downsizing*.) What benefits were there in how John D. and Lorena chose to "downsize"?

What do you admire about the Amish and how they view the elderly?

How do you feel about growing old? Are you prepared to face the next chapter in your life? Pray that God's Spirit of peace will fill your heart and thought patterns as you plan for your senior years.

PLAIN *Living*

By the time they are sixty, many Amish have accumulated enough wealth for a satisfactory retirement. Couples retire anytime between the ages of fifty and seventy. While not wealthy, income is not a serious problem.[9]

Nancy Blank's Funeral

Only one life, 'twill soon be past; only what's done for Christ will last.

Amish Proverb

Frail Nancy Blank reached the end of her life, but she didn't die alone, unnoticed. That's not the Amish way.

Bill and Jane Brenner, an English couple, live in a small Pennsylvania town. In the late 1980s, they met Nancy and soon developed a warm, give-and-take friendship. She was the Brenners' first Amish friend. "We began visiting Nancy every two to three weeks," said Bill. "We frequently took our own friends and relatives to meet her. She was so hospitable and also appreciated meeting 'our people' from time to time. She often spoke of the Lord and cited Bible references in her cards and letters."

Nancy had just turned eighty-six when the Brenners visited her in mid-February, before heading south to Florida for their annual trip. "Nancy was her own 'chipper' self," said Bill. "In late March, when we returned, we were astonished to find that her health had deteriorated. Her family said she had 'turned for the worst' soon after we left."

The Brenners kept in close contact with Nancy, stopping by to see her every day or two. "Nancy was buoyed by the birth of a new great-granddaughter—her ninety-ninth great-grandchild—whose parents, Mary and Elam, named her Nancy Lapp (Nancy's maiden name)." Bill said that Nancy had a good day when she was able to meet her little namesake, less than a week old. "Soon after, she wanted to see the baby again, so we volunteered to bring the baby and parents. We arrived mid-morning, and Nancy seemed to be aware of the baby."

Just a few hours later, as they were getting into the car to go home, Mary's mother came out to tell them that Nancy was going. They hurried back to Nancy's room. Shortly thereafter, Nancy died. The family stopped her clock in her memory. An Amish custom is to stop a person's clock at the time of death until after the burial.

Word of mouth is powerful among the Amish; news of Nancy's passing spread like rivulets of water through the community. "When the rest of her children arrived," Bill said, "the family had a time of prayer."

Then things started moving quickly. Within one hour after Nancy's death, women were in the kitchen preparing a meal for those at the house. "Men and women from her church came to prepare the house for the viewing and for the funeral in the home. In the evening, after we had viewed her body and were preparing to leave, we were told by Nancy's son, 'We want you to be part of our family.'" Deeply touched and honored to be included, the Brenners returned to the house for several hours on Saturday and Sunday.

The extended family was seated around the large room, men on one side and women on the other. As friends arrived at the house, they shook hands with each person, usually without comment, viewed Nancy's still body, and shook hands again on the way out.

The funeral was on Monday morning. "Back at Nancy's house," Bill said, "each buggy was numbered (1, 2, 3, etc.) with chalk for the processional to the cemetery. The service began about 9:00, with a full house—350 or more—seated on benches. Three preachers spoke, all in Pennsylvania Dutch. After nearly three hours we prepared for the trip to the cemetery, a processional of over forty buggies and three motor vehicles."

At the cemetery, Nancy's coffin was opened. No words were spoken and no sign was given, but everyone rose to their feet and filed by for a final tribute, to see her life-worn body one last time. After her coffin was lowered into the grave, several young men shoveled the dirt into the grave, working two by two. The earthly life of Nancy Blank had come to an end.

Final words were given by the preacher. The service did not eulogize Nancy, since the Amish hold that all praise goes to God and not individuals. That's what Nancy would have wanted: not looking backward but looking forward to eternity.

The Amish receive death gracefully, as the ultimate surrender to God's higher ways. Their strong family ties—including rituals and traditions observed so carefully throughout their lives—shine with purpose in moments like these, providing closure and comfort.

After the burial, everyone returned home. A group of women served lunch for the family members and invited guests. "We had celebrated a life well-lived for God and people," said Bill.

And Nancy's clock was reset and restarted.

Reflections on Time

The Amish do not shrug from death or avoid the reality of it. Accepting death as a natural course is a peace-giving perspective.

What are some of the ways in which obedience and remembrance are ritualized in your faith?

How do these observed rituals of the Amish bring comfort to those in grief?

What is the source of this peace in the heart of the Christian? Have you ever found peace with God through Jesus Christ?

PLAIN *Living*

When there is a death in the community, the Amish youth 16 and over will show up the evening before the funeral to sing hymns at the home where the funeral will be. As many as 300 to 500 "young folk" have shown up to sing; sometimes, the teens do not even know the deceased.[10]

Part 3

Community

Community is like an old coat—you aren't aware of it until it is taken away.

Amish Proverb

I t is a hot August afternoon in a large, dusty field in central California. Picture an enormous canvas tent, as big as a circus tent minus the stripes, and the circus. Within the tent, place long, even rows of backless benches that face the center. Fill it with hundreds of Plain People, patiently listening to the preacher, a tall wisp of a man with a horseshoe beard and thin, metal-rimmed glasses.

It feels like stepping into another century.

My mother's family, the Benedicts, members of the Old Order German Baptist Brethren Church (also known as Dunkards), have invited us to this special gathering. Every few years, a Dunkard colony takes a turn hosting a weeklong event for church members scattered around the country. The purpose of the gathering is for fellowship and worship, nothing more. Just to reinforce the ties that bind them.

We meet distant Benedict relatives, of whom there are many. My grandfather was one of eleven children. To this day, whenever I come across a Dunkard, I ask if they know of the Benedicts. Often, they *are* a Benedict.

We try not to feel as conspicuous as we look, but soon, it is obvious that the Dunkards are more comfortable with outsiders than we are with them. My family sits on a bench, like pigeons on a telephone wire, a little dazed at the setting. A song leader begins a slow, mournful hymn, a cappella, and the people repeat the refrain.

After the preaching and hymn singing, we are invited for lunch in another big tent. They insist we are guests and serve us first: slices of roast beef smothered in gravy, sweet pickles, white bread, and apple butter. And Pepsi! My Dunkard cousins love Pepsi.

I soak in the vision, the sight of these quiet, gentle people savoring their family connections. The sense of belonging is palpable. This gathering is important. They plan for it, drive long distances, cherish the opportunity for face-to-face visits with friends and relatives.

My children have never forgotten that day. Locked in their memories is the day they stepped back in time and saw—no, they *felt*—their heritage. An ordinary afternoon turned extraordinary.

Since that hot August afternoon, I have tried to host more gatherings for my extended family. Cousins play tag and climb trees in the backyard, grandparents gather in the living room, moms experiment with new recipes in the kitchen while dads sit glued to a football game on the television.

Not exactly Dunkard style but, still, we're reinforcing the ties that bind us.

Bart Township Fire Station 51

The light that shines farthest, shines brightest at home.

Amish Proverb

The little fire station in Bart, Pennsylvania, is easy to miss. It sits on a quiet street, surrounded by houses, some shops, and fields. Station 51 has one hundred volunteer firemen. Seventy-five of those are Amish. There is a siren on the side of the station to call the Amish firemen; the others have pagers.

Fire Chief Curt Woerth was raised in Bart among the Amish. "It's not like the Amish are living on an Indian reservation," he said. "The community is not divided into 'us/them,' but truly 'we.'"

He's right. The Amish overlap with the English. Cars pass by buggies, Amish women work in the tourist stops, English houses are right next to Amish ones. The only obvious difference to the casual observer is that there is no electrical wiring leading from the street to an Amish home.

There are twenty-eight Amish schools in the district surrounding Station 51. The station has a trailer in the back parking lot to teach schoolchildren about fire safety, including children from Amish one-room schoolhouses. "We found it was easier to bus the students to the station than to try to find an appropriate place to park the trailer at each of the twenty-eight little school sites," explained Woerth.

One of those little schools was the West Nickel Mines School.

When the tragic disaster of the shootings at the West Nickel Mines School struck this community on October 2, 2006, the Bart Township Fire Company was the first on the scene to respond. Within hours, the station house became the central command hub. To meet the community's needs, Station 51 workers were put out of service for a week beginning at 2 p.m. after the shootings; their calls were covered by the other local fire stations.

Over the next week, the Ladies Auxiliary of the Fire Company provided three meals a day to all firefighters, EMS, law enforcement, and the Amish families of those involved. "The fire station was a safe haven for everyone," said Woerth. "It was a whole community effort. Local vendors, like Wal-mart and Costco, sent jiffy johns, toilet paper, paper plates, paper cups. All the meals were served at the station—eight hundred to nine hundred meals during the time of the funerals. One guy came every day just to clean the toilets. He knew it needed to be done, and he found a way to help."

Counseling, provided by local hospitals, was set up at the fire station for any and all who needed it. Many of the Amish families were able to benefit from the counseling, Woerth pointed out.

Hundreds of packages and thousands of letters flowed through the fire station. All packages and letters were sorted and checked before being distributed to the families. "All the mountains of mail received were opened by five ladies who sorted every piece." Part of that precaution was for protection. Hard to believe, but some hate mail was sent to the Amish families.

Woerth said the fire station had never dealt with this type of thing before, especially all the media. "Really, 95 percent of the media was good, very respectful. It was just a couple who made things more difficult." He's referring to one reporter, in particular, who disguised herself as an Amish woman and tried to sneak into a funeral.

There has been no annual memorial remembrance of October 2. "Life will never return to what it was before," said Woerth. "We have also learned through this tragic event that we live in a community where people care about one another and put the needs of others first."

Woerth knew some of the victims. "One of the girls who was killed, Naomi Rose, had baked a pumpkin pie and brought it to my mother the night before the shooting," he said. "My mom had cancer and was going in for chemotherapy the next morning. She was actually getting her chemo treatment when she saw the news on the TV. She was devastated."

In countless ways, the police, civic officials, and Amish worked hand in hand to respond to the tragic event in the days and months that followed. When Lancaster County honored the first responders—firefighters, state troopers, investigators—in an official proclamation, no one was singled out as a hero to be recognized. They were united that day and wanted to be recognized as a team. "The police, fire, and EMS only did what they are trained to do. The difference with this situation was the watchful eye of the media."

Chief Woerth dropped his chin to his chest for a moment, then lifted it a notch. "The only true heroes that day were the children in the school."

REFLECTIONS ON COMMUNITY

What tragedy has your community encountered, and how did you and others respond? What did it teach you about where you look for security?

In September 2008, just before Hurricane Ike hit Houston, Texas, one neighbor bought walkie-talkies for everyone on his street to be able to communicate with each other in case they lost power. A sense of loss and need can bring people together. What are some ways to create a caring community—church or neighborhood—*before* a crisis hits?

How can faith in the sovereignty of God give you confidence as you face difficulties in your life?

PLAIN *Living*

Ten days after the West Nickel Mines School shooting occurred, before dawn, a large backhoe tore into the overhang of the schoolhouse. Large construction spotlights glared in the mist as the backhoe knocked down the bell tower and toppled the walls. Fifteen minutes later, the one-room schoolhouse was reduced to a pile of rubble.

The local Amish elders felt it was best to remove the schoolhouse. They were concerned about tourists converging on the site, creating a memorial, or turning it into a tourist site. All week long, people had been leaving flowers and notes and balloons and teddy bears. Every few hours, an Amish neighbor would scoop the gifts up and take them to the fire station to be distributed to children in need.

As neighborhood children finished up their breakfasts and left home for school, the debris was removed, hauled away by dump trucks. By the end of the school day, the field had been plowed and re-seeded. The footprint of the West Nickel Mines one-room schoolhouse was entirely gone. By sunset, it looked like any other pasture.

Artist Susie Riehl

The Goldenrod yellow and Chicory blossoms blue,
The Lord has created, to benefit you.

Amish Proverb

When Susie Lapp was in sixth grade, Anna Weaver arrived as her new teacher at the one-room schoolhouse in Myerstown, Pennsylvania. "Anna let us do more than freehand drawing," Susie said. "She showed us how to mix colors. How to observe nature. She taught me that drawing is in the eye, not in the hand." When Susie graduated eighth grade, Anna gave her a watercolor set. "She gave all of the children little gifts. For me, it was a box of twenty-seven colors with a brush. It felt like a promise that my art didn't have to stop just because school stopped. For most of the Amish, art for art's sake does stop."

At home, Susie sketched houses, farms, and barns, continuing to experiment. With books checked out from the library, she taught herself new skills. Such self-initiative is an Amish trait; she thinks it stems from their strong work ethic. "We're taught to think. We learn to make do with what we have," she said. "We can't just go buy things. We have to figure things out for ourselves."

Susie's parents encouraged and supported her painting. After marrying John Riehl, a farmer, the couple adopted two children, then had four biological ones. With bills from four Caesarean sections, John and Susie needed income to hold on to the farm. So

Susie painted. Her studio was the kitchen table, her office hours consisted of moments snatched between chores. "I painted a lot while the children were small. Now, they're older and I don't have as much time. I think it's good to find a place to make yourself a haven, to block out the jabbering and the noise. But I was always careful to go look when the children got too quiet!"

Susie's trademark is watercolors of quilts. "I saw a quilt hanging on a clothesline and thought to myself, 'Now that would make a good painting.' Quilts were something I knew. I grew up making them and understood their patterns. It occurred to me to paint quilts in different settings."

About that time in her life, she was introduced to photographer Shirley Wenger. Susie asked Shirley to photograph her subjects— quilts in settings around farms—so she could study them to paint. Shirley also helped to commercialize Susie's work by hanging her paintings in the Wenger Gallery and printing note cards from the original watercolors.

Susie gives her painting a great deal of thought before actually sitting down to paint it. "I think about it a lot as I go about my chores. I imagine it in my mind." Watercolors aren't as forgiving as oils; a mistake means a start over. "But it's not as expensive as oils, either." The entire process, to Susie, is just as valuable as the end result. "But don't ever think the Amish are perfect!" Susie said, laughing. "We all have a tendency to rush through things. But it doesn't pay. It just means mistakes. We all need to slow down more, hang out the wash, and listen to the birds. To enjoy every moment."

Susie paints for the glory of God. "It's the only way I can do it," she said. "It all comes from him." She once read that a Christian can be an artist but never a great artist. "I agree with that. We can't let a talent God gave us take the place God should have in our life. We can't let it be an obsession. It always has to be God, first."

One of the by-products Susie has developed through her artwork is a great appreciation for God's creation through the subtleties of nature. "Once, I painted a head of cabbage. Something as simple as that. In the garden, I studied a real cabbage and discovered so many shades of green!" Susie has developed such a skilled eye that she doesn't need the photographs to study as much as she used to. "In my mind's eye, I get the shadows. Of course," she was quick to point out, "the paintings are not perfect."

Susie hasn't painted much in the last few years. She has had daughters' weddings to plan, and now grandchildren are starting to arrive. "Family takes time. They need my help. We're even canning more since grocery prices are rising. I have hardly painted at all, but maybe next year."

Doesn't the commercialization of Susie's artwork make her stand out as an individual? And wouldn't that make it in conflict with Amish beliefs? "I'm not quite sure how I get away with it," Susie admitted. "But I think making pictures of quilts keeps it within the boundaries."

Still, Susie has struggled with the priority painting has in her life. "I gave up painting for a while—I became too obsessed with it. I caught myself sometimes—feeling as if I was 'living to paint.' I love painting but I don't want it to become too important. It's a way of expressing things for me, and it gives me a lot of excitement, a lot of joy. The feeling goes deep, deeper than what I ever thought it would. But it isn't the meaning of my life. I sometimes ask myself, 'Have I put too much of my life into painting? And not enough into spiritual things?'" She paused. "After all, in our faith, we have something worth taking care of."

REFLECTIONS ON COMMUNITY

Who encouraged you the most when you were young? In what way? If you haven't done so already, consider sharing with that person how she or he blessed you.

Which of God's blessings do you especially appreciate?

What talent has God given you? Have you been ignoring it?

PLAIN *Living*

An Amish person often has more than seventy-five first cousins. A typical grandmother may count as many as fifty grandchildren.[1]

The Lowly Spirit of *Gelassenheit*

Swallowing pride rarely gives you indigestion.

Amish Proverb

Cora met Mary Ellen, her sister, at the kitchen door of the farmhouse. "Where have you been?" she asked.

Mary Ellen hung her black bonnet upside down on the wall peg in the kitchen. "It's a long story," she sighed, as she pulled out a kitchen chair and sat down wearily.

Cora put the kettle on the stovetop to boil water for tea. The telling of a story, like so many other things in this life, was always made better by a cup of tea.

Mary Ellen explained that she had just returned from a visit to Lovina, a woman in her district who was recently diagnosed with cancer. It wasn't an easy visit, but not for the obvious reason. Though it seems like an oxymoron in an Amish community that emphasizes confession and forgiveness, Lovina is a woman who hangs on to her grudges. She creates conflicts between herself and others; in fact, she seems to thrive on conflict.

Cora handed Mary Ellen a cup of hot tea. "Did you see any change of heart?"

Mary Ellen shook her head. "Not really. Same as always." She blew across the rim of her cup to cool the tea. A small wisp of steam rose up, then vanished. "She brought it up again."

"What?! That happened fifty years ago." Cora frowned. "That woman nurses her grudges like some folks baby their roses."

Fifty years ago, Lovina's brother had been sweet on Mary Ellen, but she didn't return his interest and eventually married someone else. Lovina had never forgiven Mary Ellen, calling her proud and vain.

"She makes it hard, so hard, to be friendly to her," Mary Ellen said. She wrestled with feeling any compassion for Lovina. But she would continue to try to reach out to her with love and acceptance, expecting nothing in return. It's what Mary Ellen was raised to do. It's what she needed to do. It's not the easy road, but that's what *Gelassenheit* is all about.

Gelassenheit is a foundational value in Amish society that has no direct English translation. The best way to understand the richness of its meaning, said Durand Overholtzer, an Anabaptist minister, is through synonyms: yieldedness, humility, calmness, composure, meekness, aplomb, tranquility, imperturbability, serenity, poise, sedateness, letting go, the opposite of self-assertion, a gentle spirit, submitting to God's will. "It is the union and agreement of the inner spirit with the outward response," he explained. "Christ is the best example of Gelassenheit. He provided the ultimate example of it when he, the Creator, yielded his life for the created."

Gelassenheit is caught, not taught. The very first thing Amish children learn is that there is always a higher authority to yield to—older siblings, parents and grandparents, the greater good of the community, and God. Obedience tops the list of what Amish parents want their children to learn, beginning with teaching little ones to fold their hands in prayer for grace before a meal—the first step in expressing thankfulness to God. And, to the Plain way of thinking, one never outgrows the commandment to obey parents.

Gelassenheit stresses humility over pride and esteems others above self. "It means helping others, never doing it for brownie points, never trying to get something for yourself in return," explained an Old Order Amish bishop. "It means that I am surrendering my will to God. Every day, in every way. It's not just knowing the will of God, it's *doing* it."

The hard things, he means. Turning the other cheek, blessing your enemy, getting rid of sinful habits, giving sacrificially, loving the unlovable. All of the things Christ referred to in the Sermon on the Mount.

The Amish place great spiritual and social significance on the Lord's Prayer (Matthew 6) and on the Sermon of the Mount (Matthew 5–7) in Amish worship, life, and faith. "Gelassenheit is why the Sermon on the Mount is favored by the Anabaptists," said the minister.

Unlike mainstream Protestantism, which views God's grace as free and unending, the Amish believe there are some strings attached to God's grace and forgiveness—namely, passing on the forgiveness to others. "If grace covers all," asked the bishop, "why bother being Plain?"

The two verses that follow the Lord's Prayer, where Jesus says (in essence), "If you don't forgive, you won't be forgiven," are central to Amish faith and practice. "That's what it [the Sermon on the Mount] is all about," said the bishop.

It's hard to understand that Lovina's habit of nursing grudges is tolerated. It would be a mistake, though, to think that just because the Amish dress alike, look alike, and live alike, that they also think alike. They are the first to tell you they are not perfect people. Lovina may never change, but Mary Ellen will keep on visiting and extending friendship to her, as unpleasant as those visits are for her. "It's my cross to bear," Mary Ellen told Cora. She swallowed the last sip of tea and handed the empty cup to her sister. "Someday, maybe, with God's help, she will change."

"Yes, of course you're right," said Cora, as she made her sister another cup of tea. She could see that just talking this over had restored her sister's spirits, and a cup of tea helped do the rest.

REFLECTIONS ON COMMUNITY

Is Gelassenheit an Amish value? Or a Christian value? When have you seen an example of Gelassenheit in your community? In the world?

Is Gelassenheit something all Christians should aspire to?

If you took the spirit of Gelassenheit to heart, what would change in your life?

PLAIN *Living*

"To truly understand the Amish," says Donald B. Kraybill, "you have to understand the central value of Gelassenheit. It means giving up self to community. Everything flows from that basic concept. Most Americans really wouldn't want Gelassenheit. To a typical American, the individual comes first. To the Amish, the community comes first."[2]

God's Special Children

It isn't the mountains ahead that wear you out, it's the grain of sand in your shoe.

Amish Proverb

John and Mary King have nine children. Their youngest, Sallie, is a twenty-year-old slender reed of a girl who looks closer to ten, born with physical and mental handicaps. Sallie has an inherited genetic disorder. She is severely disabled, unable to control her body or communicate other than in grunts.

The entire family adores Sallie. Everyone lends a hand in her constant care. They take her everywhere they go, including church. They're very accustomed to and tolerant of Sallie's odd noises and jerky movements. While talking to a visitor, Mary wraps her arms around Sallie to gently control her movements, never missing a beat of the conversation. John holds Sallie to feed her. In fact, all of her siblings lovingly touch her and hug her as an important and valued member of their family. Like a laying on of hands, all throughout the day.

Sallie will always have a place at home with John and Mary. The Amish care for their disabled and infirm at home. In the Amish world there is a tolerance and compassion for those who are impaired. The community tries to provide a sense of belonging and of being needed. Handicapped children and adults are not considered a social problem, for an individual's worth is not measured by performance. Just the opposite. "We have learned so much from Sallie," says Mary. "She's taught us how to love others. She's given us an opportunity to express love." In *The Budget*, obituaries of children with genetic diseases refer to them as "one of God's special children."

Two days a week, Sallie attends a day care program at the world-renowned Clinic for Special Children located in nearby Strasburg, Pennsylvania. The clinic was founded in 1989 by pediatrician and geneticist Dr. D. Holmes Morton, with Caroline, his wife, who is the executive director of the clinic. The clinic sits in the middle of farmland owned by the Amish grandparents of some of the first children whose illnesses Dr. Morton diagnosed. They sold it to him at less than half the market price. Dr. Morton refused to take tillable farmland and chose a few wooded acres as the building site.

The clinic is a post-and-beam style Amish barn, held together by pegs. Indeed, it was "raised" by Amish and Mennonite carpenters in one day, on a blustery November afternoon. Inside is state-of-the-art technology, some of the finest in the world. It's said to be the only place in the country with a mass spectrometer inside (an expensive but essential machine to screen newborns that was donated by David Packard of Hewlett-Packard) . . . and a hitching post outside.

The Clinic for Special Children has become a very important resource for the Amish and Mennonite communities. During the year, auctions are held by hundreds of volunteers from Amish and Mennonite communities, who provide quilts and other items for the sale, including preparing and serving food. These events raise nearly a third of the clinic's annual $1.2 million operating budget. As a result, the clinic is able to charge very little for its services, including its day care center. "At eleven o'clock, Dr. Morton gives a speech," says Esther Smucker, whose relative works at the clinic. "Everyone at the auction stops what they are doing to hear him. It's always very touching."

Clearly, Dr. Morton is beloved. "He's an amazing man," Esther adds. "He's been such a blessing."

D. Holmes Morton is somewhat of a maverick, complete with a signature red bowtie around his neck and a cello by his side. A lover of classical string music, he decided to learn to play the cello at age fifty and tackled it with the same determination as chasing down a defective gene. He was awarded the Albert Schweitzer Prize for Humanitarianism in 1993. While not of Anabaptist descent, he does share some beliefs: he doesn't bother with the traditional means of financing medical projects, such as government grants. And he believes each child—perfect gene code or not—is special.

REFLECTIONS ON COMMUNITY

Are there any handicapped, impaired, or even elderly people in your lives? What have you learned from them?

Scripture states that God "will take pity on the weak and the needy" (Ps. 72:13) and "blessed is he who has regard for the weak" (Ps. 41:1). How would you describe God's point of view about children like Sallie?

How does a belief in eternal life give you peace about some of life's apparent inequalities?

PLAIN *Living*

There are basically only fifty or so different last names among the Amish.[3]

Help Thy Neighbor

Do unto others as if you were the other.

Amish Proverb

On the very day that Willis Schrock, a forty-something farmer with a craggy face and a bumpy nose, decided his oats were ripe for harvest, the sharp pain in his abdomen developed into a full-blown ruptured appendix. By that evening, he had undergone emergency surgery. As soon as he woke up in the recovery room, he looked at his wife, Marianne, his gray eyes round as silver dollars. "Help me get dressed and get home!" he told her. "The oats have to be shocked."

Of course, Marianne wasn't about to help an injured, weakened, stubborn man in a hospital bed make a getaway. "Neighbors arrived and did all of the work for us," she said, sweeping her arm in a broad arc, and then folding it up against her chest, as if she was gathering that memory to her heart for safekeeping. "It touched me deeply to realize anew how dependent we are upon our people."

As one neighbor cut the oats, another one shocked them. When one team of horses tired, another neighbor brought along his four-horse team. Marianne said that when they were just about done with the fields, the men called Willis's young children to come and watch. "So the art of shocking oats can be passed down to our children," she said, pleased. "It was a beautiful evening. As the shocks were being set up, a coyote was yipping only a short distance away. We ended the day with roasted hot dogs around a campfire as the sun set. Tired but happy."

Not much later, the very neighbor who was first to help Willis when he was in the hospital needed help in return. "He had an accident and was stuck in the hospital for a week," Willis explained. "So the neighbors brought their teams and mowers to cut his acreage of alfalfa hay. With three teams and wagons and two hay loaders, we had the hay in his barn in just a few hours."

Satisfied with their work, the men rested under the shade of an elm tree with lemonade and fresh cookies provided by Marianne, swapping stories and jokes. "Depending on others is usually seen as a weakness," said Marianne. "But to us, to our way of thinking, depending on others is a strength."

Harvest time means pitching in to gather crops. "One late June afternoon," Willis remembered, "a soaker [heavy rainfall] was due in. My sons and I went from farm to farm to help neighbors collect hay from the field and move it into their barns. We returned home tired but happy. The crops were safe."

Marianne pointed to a biblical principle expressed in how their neighbors helped each other. "When Willis was in the hospital, I could just see so clearly the fruits of the Spirit in action, all done in love. If people had only come and wished us well, that alone would not have done the work. Faith and works go hand in hand."

The Amish take care of their own. Twice a year money is collected for the widows and others who are unable to earn a living. Those biannual offerings are the only time the plate is passed in church. Said one Amish farmer, "People don't need more insurance. They need assurance. Assurance of a God who loves them. And of neighbors who will help them get back on their feet."

The barn raising is symbolic of the ways that the Amish maintain their sense of community. Some have had as many as 600 persons in attendance. Word of mouth, a mighty power among the Amish, spreads the details of a barn raising. Neighbors share the news, it's announced in area churches, women organize the noon meal and send out letters to their extended families about specific foods and amounts to bring. It all comes together, without a single email. A non-technological wonder.

Weddings and funerals, attended by 300 to 400 people, are also symbolic of Amish community. Neighbors provide hands-on help in the form of food preparation, house cleaning, hostelling the horses and buggies, and cleaning up afterward. "There's no such thing as a small wedding or funeral," laughs a grandmother. "We have *families!*"

After attending their first Amish wedding, one English couple was amazed at the seamless coordination of efforts. "After the ceremony, it took less than half an hour to transform the room for serving lunch," said the English husband. "We ate family style in three 'shifts,' with the dishes cleared, washed, and re-set very quickly. That afternoon, we sat on benches and sang their traditional wedding hymns and songs. During this time, many kinds of foods were passed around for snacking. After a break, we prepared for the wedding dinner, which was again served in shifts. The wedding began at eight in the morning; we left about seven thirty in the evening." Like so much that's Amish, it was plain and simple and satisfying.

An Amish family can be recovering from an unexpected disaster, raising a barn, burying a loved one, or celebrating a marriage, but it will never be alone.

REFLECTIONS ON COMMUNITY

Marianne said that the Amish consider depending on others to be a strength. Do you see dependence on others as a weakness or a strength?

Do you allow yourself to be inconvenienced by the needs of others? What have you learned about sharing with others in need?

What is God's Spirit leading you to do in relationship to other people?

PLAIN *Living*

An Amish couple keeps their wedding plans secret, except for close family and friends, until the announcement is made at church.[4]

I Like to Put My Feet under the Table

Trusting God turns problems into opportunities.

Amish Proverb

When Sam Lapp decided to marry Amanda, his sweetheart, his father helped him buy a farm. Sam felt blessed; many of his friends had to work off the farm to make a living. A year after their wedding, Sam and Amanda had their first child, a little girl named Hannah. Sam looks forward to raising Hannah—and hopefully to adding a few brothers and sisters—on the farm. "There's no better place to raise children," he said. "Farm living teaches them all about life."

Not long ago, Sam was helping to erect an outbuilding at his neighbor's farm. Amanda went along with him and helped prepare lunch in the farmhouse. About midway through the afternoon, Sam burst into the kitchen. Amanda sprang to her feet, worried that there had been an accident. Sam scooped baby Hannah from his wife's arms. "There she is! I haven't held her all day." That was all he wanted. A baby fix.

If a mother is the heart of the Amish life, the father is the head; he plays a very significant role, spiritually and practically, in his family. Being a hands-on dad is of paramount importance to Amish men. Raising children is not considered women's work; it is a shared task. In church, sons sit by their fathers; girls and infants with their mothers. A father mentors his children by teaching them how to farm. Driving through the back roads of Amish America, a sight to behold is an Amish father with his toddler son on his lap, large hands covering small ones that hold the reins, guiding two harnessed mules that pull a heavy plow. Another common sight is an Amish father with a child, in the middle of the day, running errands in the buggy or on a scooter.

To an Amish father like Sam, the context of his daily life revolves around home. A home means so much more to Sam than a roof and a mortgage. Every part of his life—all that is significant to him— centers there: Hannah was born at home, helped by a midwife. She will attend school within walking distance of home. One day, her wedding will take place at home. Sam and Amanda's farm is within a few miles of their childhood homes—a geographical and familial tie to this land. When Sam works in the fields and in the barn, he is within shouting distance of the farmhouse. It's like he is tethered, willingly and happily, to it.

There's a saying among Amish men: "I like to put my feet under the table." It means that fathers want to have three meals a day at home, surrounded by their families. Most of the family's meals are eaten at home, with each member in their place at the same spot, every day. It's a symbol of belonging. Sam's place is at the head of the table, Amanda sits next to him, the baby next to her. "When a place is vacant due to death, marriage, sickness, father's having gone to town, the discipline of the ban, or a runaway child, all are deeply aware of the empty place," wrote John Hostetler in *Amish Society*.[5]

The shift away from farming because of shrinking farmland is considered one of the most important changes that have taken place in Amish society in the twentieth century. It threatens their entire way of life by taking the father away from the home. Church leaders worry that fathers, stuck in a 9-to-5 schedule, will be less successful in passing on the Amish way of life to the next generation. "We were brought up by our parents to be Amish," Sam said.

"The whole idea is, we teach by example." He shrugged. "How can you do that when you're not home?"

Sideline businesses, where family members work together in a shop on the property, have become common practice in the Amish community. "The next best thing to being a farmer," Sam said, "is a cottage business." Fathers and sons work in trades that do everything from cabinetmaking to blacksmithing. "We'll do whatever we can to stay home and keep the family together." Because fatherhood, to Sam and to all Plain People, is the most important role in a man's life.

REFLECTIONS ON COMMUNITY

Sam sees himself first as a father, second as a farmer. Does the way he values his role put fatherhood in a new light for you?

Being Amish means that family life—just being together—is highly valued. What are some ways your family spends time together?

Do you wish your family had more time together? It's never too late. Today, look for a small way for your family to enjoy spending time together—a special dessert, a board game, or a walk with the dog.

PLAIN *Living*

Today roughly half of the Amish households are engaged in farming. Of the three main settlements, Ohio has the largest percentage of non-farmers. Very few of the Amish household heads work as farm laborers.[6]

One-Room Schoolhouse

It is better to hold out a helping hand than to point a finger.

Amish Proverb

L izzie and Timmy's lives are about to change. The five-year-old twins have spent their days at home, playing in the tree fort built by their dad. They've already learned to do chores— feeding the chickens, raking the garden so their mom can plant the summer vegetables. Mostly, though, they play. They have a stick farm that, from a distance, almost looks like rows of asparagus. It delights Alice, their mom. "I think Amish children might use their imagination more than English children," Alice said, watching her children hammer another row of sticks into the hard-packed soil. "Don't get me wrong. They have plenty of toys. But they use their creativity."

Soon, Lizzie and Timmy will join their four older siblings as "scholars" and attend the one-room schoolhouse just a stone's throw from their farm. In the spring, they'll go to school for a few weeks, to start to get comfortable with the routine. Alice is a little hesitant about Timmy. "I'm just not sure he's ready yet," she said, her face scrunched up in worry, looking like any mother of a five-year-old boy.

Lizzie and Timmy know some English from hearing their older brothers and sisters speak, but Pennsylvania Dutch is their first language. Classes are taught only in English for the first three years, and then German grammar is introduced.

The school is visible from Lizzie and Timmy's house. The land was donated by an Amish neighbor and sits on the corner of his farm, close to the road. The schoolhouse is well constructed, made of stucco and wood, painted pale yellow, with an old-fashioned rope-pulled school bell on top. Out in front is a pump that allows for well water. A cinderblock outhouse edges one corner of the yard. The schoolyard is wide and square, big enough for a ball field but empty of play equipment. It is here that the study of nature and language and music and arithmetic and softball blend together to become one.

Inside, the atmosphere is simple but charming. Large windows allow for natural lighting. The rows of old-fashioned wooden desks are named after flowers: Lilac Lane, Sunflower Road. Cheerful children's artwork hangs on the walls. Bible verses rim the edge of the ceiling, like a wall relief. The air smells of freshly oiled wood floors.

To mainstream Americans who place a premium on higher education, an Amish education might raise an eyebrow. To our way of thinking, it might seem limited and restrictive. Unmarried young Amish women—without college training—teach in small parochial schools. Amish schools use a limited amount of material in the classroom—they have created their own readers, workbooks, and texts. They stress accuracy rather than speed, drill rather than variety, proper sequence rather than critical thinking skills. And formal schooling ends at the eighth grade.

Yet illiteracy is virtually nonexistent in Amish settlements. Without television and computers, the Amish read more than most Americans. They have a remarkable ability to learn new skills—even complicated ones—and value lifelong learning. Amish communities believe their schools should teach the same thing as the home and the church—emphasizing Christian virtues of honesty, obedience, reverence, decency, discipline. Amish parents are heavily involved in their children's education: they donate the land and building supplies for the school, visit regularly, attend school events, and take turns caring for the facilities.

In *Amish Society*, author John Hostetler wrote, "On several standardized tests, Amish children performed significantly higher in spelling, word usage, and arithmetic than a sample of pupils in rural public schools. They scored slightly above the national norm in these subjects in spite of small libraries, limited equipment, the absence of radio and television, and teachers who lacked college training."[7]

But most gratifying to the community: Amish children in the eighth grade gave a more positive rating to their families than did non-Amish children.

REFLECTIONS ON COMMUNITY

How involved is your entire community in the education of its children? Think of ways to get involved that will lead children to take their place in the wider world.

What are some ways your community is involved in the education of its children? How do those involvements help knit a community together? What benefits occur when a community takes responsibility for each other?

The Amish emphasize learning topics thoroughly. They value accuracy over speed, quality over quantity. Doing something well is highly valued and is a source of great satisfaction. What are some ways you can encourage your children to do their personal best?

How would you define a lifelong learner? Do you consider yourself to be one?

How can you be a better example of that to your children?

PLAIN *Living*

By not entering high school, Amish children are all classed as dropouts in public school statistics.[8]

Children Are Loved but Not Adored

It is the set of the sails and not the gales that determines the path you go.

Amish Proverb

Amish children are loved but not adored. Wanted but not made to feel special. Provided for but not spoiled.

Dr. Ervin Stutzman, dean of Eastern Mennonite Seminary, was born into an Old Order Amish family. "As I reflect on my growing up years, my childhood was a huge gift," he said. "I never wondered if I was needed or wanted as a child." Children are very important in the Amish culture. Stutzman never knew of a time when the birth of a child was an unwelcomed event.

Stutzman's father, Tobias, was killed in an accident when the boy was only three years old. His older brother and an uncle stepped up as father figures. "They kept me in line."

To the Amish, children are blessings from the Lord. The average family has seven children, but ten or more is not uncommon. Children are not only loved and wanted but necessary to help with farm work. They are an Amish family's strength, life, and perpetuity.

Amish babies and toddlers are showered with love and attention. They are thoroughly enjoyed by the entire family and included in all activities, including meals. If a baby cries, he needs comfort, not discipline.

"There's great value given to children socially in the Amish church," said Stutzman. "They're seen as assets, not liabilities. They're celebrated, valued, and sought after. In the English community, we use birth control because we don't want children. The Amish view children very differently. They're seen as a help to the family, as a part of a whole. In fact, as a general rule in the community, children and teens work and give income to their parents until they are twenty-one."

The very first thing Amish children learn is there is always a higher authority to yield to—whether it's parents, church, or God. "Amish children are not indulged," said Stutzman. "Spiritually, parenting is a huge privilege and responsibility. That's how children are shaped. Children are taught to obey their parents. When a child has a temper tantrum, it's a reflection on the parenting. It's seen as poor parenting. We were disciplined, made to behave. We weren't raised being told that we're special."

As hard as they work, the Amish allow their children to have remarkable freedom. "We had an emotionally safe childhood," Stutzman recalled. "My mother didn't have to worry that I was getting into drugs or alcohol. We had the run of the farm. I had huge freedom compared to most children today. I could roam anywhere. There was a village looking out for children."

Amish youth grow up in a thick web of family. As one Plain grandmother put it, "I know these children. Everyone does. I know every face that passes my house on a scooter. I know where they are going and when and why."

Stutzman admitted that while his childhood was emotionally safe, it might not have been physically safe. "We were without parental supervision. Amish children are exposed to a lot of danger on a farm. An eight-year-old does a man's work—such as driving a team of horses. I remember accidents from using large farm equipment.

The emergency wards see a high rate of accidents among Amish children. It might not have been physically safe. But we felt safe."

Though not a member of the Amish church now, Stutzman has a deep regard for his people and fond memories of his upbringing. "At its highest ideal, there's just no better childhood than an Amish one."

REFLECTIONS ON COMMUNITY

How can we love our children but not make them the entire focus of our lives? How can seeing them in the context of a larger community—of family, extended family, and neighborhood—help them feel secure, which leads to greater peace?

Letting go, it seems, is part of the parenting package. How does it help to be reminded that your children belong to the Lord? "God will not reveal His plans and purposes for our approval," wrote Esther Smucker in *Good Night, My Son.* "But we must not forget that He is God."[9]

PLAIN *Living*

An Amish boy will begin to harness a horse himself and drive buggies short distances as soon as he is tall enough to do the job, perhaps ten years old.[10]

The Grocery Shower

Kindness, when given away, keeps coming back.

Amish Proverb

Scattered throughout farms in Amish America are small bulk grocery stores. They have no signage, no advertisements, no large neon lights. Only a sharp-eyed observer might notice a few metal grocery carts stacked out front and realize they belong to a store.

Inside, a stream of Amish customers quietly push their carts up and down the aisles. The store is not crowded but never empty. There's a library hush covering it, like a morning fog. A few English tourists ooh and aah over the low prices of spices. Ground cinnamon in a pint-sized container costs only twenty-five cents. An older Amish man reviews his wife's handwritten list in his hand, scratches his head, then peers up at the boxed cereals. "There it is! I just love Post Bran Flakes," he says aloud, pleased. "Best cereal on the market." Two women, good friends, meet up in an aisle, whispering news of their families.

Long metal shelving is filled with staples such as sugar, salt, flour, and lots and lots of bulk candy. There's another distinctive feature in this simple store. A cardboard box, placed near the register, with a handwritten sign on its front: "Grocery Shower. For Sam and Maryann Stoltzfus. Maryann has had two surgeries for gall bladders. Expenses are high. Let's help."

Rebecca, whose family runs this village store, explains it is an Amish custom to have a grocery shower box. "It's a way we have of taking care of our own. There's always someone who needs a little extra help." The box is overflowing with goods.

"Tomorrow," Rebecca adds, "there will be another box. Just learned of a couple whose baby was born a preemie." She said that in most communities, a week or so after a wedding, friends have a grocery shower to help fill the couple's pantry.

Caring for each other provides great security and peace of mind for church members. The Amish believe their actions of kindness are much more important than words or money.

Contrary to beliefs, the Amish are not exclusive in their care or in whom they perceive as a neighbor. Amish folks readily help their non-Amish neighbors in times of disaster, fire, or illness. "My neighbor is my neighbor whether he attends my church or is a nonbeliever," says Will, Rebecca's husband. "I help him and he helps me. We need each other."

In some communities, like Will's, Amish men actively participate in volunteer fire companies. In fact, more than half the members of some Lancaster County fire companies are Amish. The Amish also support fire companies through their public benefit auctions, which can have annual sales topping several hundred thousand dollars.

When a natural disaster strikes, the Amish reach into their pockets and give, but they also give with their time. Lancaster's Amish made many trips to assist in the reconstruction of homes in Mississippi following Hurricane Katrina in 2005. One English woman remarked that the Amish carpentry crews had such a reputation for excellent work that homeowners in Pass Christian, Mississippi, asked for them specifically to rebuild their houses.

"I've gone down to Pass Christian a couple of times," says twenty-five-year-old Joshua, a single Amish young man who lives on his family's dairy farm in Groffdale, Pennsylvania. "A busload of us go down there, for weeks at a time. I like to go, like helping out. It's fun to see a different place."

Just as important, the Amish are comfortable about making needs known. Every week, *The Budget* runs advertisements for those in need. The family is identified, the need is stated, and an address for donations is provided. The tone in the request is similar to how one would write a sister or an aunt, filling her in on a family crisis, familiar enough to ask for help.

There is a childlike trust implied in these requests. Even though the Amish are known for their frugality, they are generous with others in need. "It's because we know that someday, we might face hardships ourselves," says Rebecca. "The rain falls on the just and the unjust."

A suspicious, hardened English mind might worry that the Amish, in their naiveté and innocence, could be taken advantage of, scammed by con-artists. When such a concern was posed to Rebecca, she had a puzzled look on her face, as if she couldn't quite get her mind around such an outrageous thought. "You mean, ask for money when they don't really need it? But why? Why would someone ever do that?"

Why, indeed?

REFLECTIONS ON COMMUNITY

What motivates you to give? Is your first response to a need "why did this happen?" or "how can I help?"

Today, be as willing to share a need as fill it.

If you are part of a small group, how could you reach out as a group to show love and care for other people?

PLAIN *Living*

The Budget dedicates a weekly column to "Showers" and "Cards of Thanks." An example from a recent issue: "Let's have a get well sticker and money shower for Rhoda, 7 years old. She broke her leg while riding her bike. Her mom is a widow. Address is: . . ."

Face-to-Face

A friend is like a rainbow, always there for you after a storm.

Amish Proverb

Late Saturday afternoon, Ida Mae Miller filled up a brown bag with asparagus, freshly picked from her garden, and walked down the lane to visit Ruthie Yoder, her nearest neighbor and dearest friend. In keeping with Amish tradition, Ida Mae opened Ruthie's kitchen door and walked in, calling out Ruthie's name. Too late, she noticed that Ruthie had just finished washing the linoleum floor. It was still wet and slick; behind Ida Mae was a trail of garden mud tracked in by her bare feet.

"Oh dear," Ida Mae said, frowning, brown eyes bright in her round face. "You've just cleaned house, and here I come with my dirty feet, messing it up again."

Ruthie smiled when she saw her friend, tossed the rags into the sink, and hurried to greet Ida Mae. "Just gives me the fun of cleaning it again."

Fun?

Not many would describe scrubbing a floor for the second time as fun, but Ruthie was entirely sincere. She was delighted to have a visitor, even if it meant more work. The Amish have mastered the art of visiting, so much a part of their culture that it's been dubbed the Amish Sport. Relatives and friends visit without receiving an invitation or giving advance notice or even knocking on the door. Family and neighbors just help themselves and walk right in.

Ida Mae grabbed a rag and helped Ruthie finish washing the floor. Their talking carried on while the work was getting done. It's customary to lend a hand with whatever chores are being attended to at that moment. The saying, "A woman's work is never done," probably was coined among the Amish. Farm life keeps an Amish housewife constantly "choring." Whenever women get together, they usually take something that needs sewing or mending. One can visit, they think, and still make use of the hands. Group work helps make the time go faster, the task less tedious, and the work easier.

Visiting is so important that it is given the most coverage in the weekly Amish newspaper, *The Budget*, with observations about weather trailing in second place. When Ida Mae's daughter, Marion, spent the winter working in a coffee shop in Pinecraft, an Amish settlement in Florida, a scribe mentioned her visit in his weekly letter.

Since Ruthie was widowed last year, she likes to spend her Sunday afternoons visiting those who are ill or shut-in. "It cheers folks up to have a visitor," she said. "It means you care about them." Sympathy and compassion, for the Amish, come with a visit.

One of the main reasons that the Amish banned the telephone—around 1910 when it became common to have them in the home—was to safeguard the practice of face-to-face visits. The Amish bishops recognized that the telephone was not merely a neutral instrument but could tie church members directly to the outside world. Having a telephone inside the home would allow others to interrupt family life. However, the *use* of the telephone was never forbidden. In the 1940s, community phones were permitted in unheated telephone shanties at the end of farm lanes. These community phones, shared by several families, were primarily used for outgoing, rather than incoming, calls. The Amish believe that talking face-to-face is far superior to phone conversation.

As Ruthie said, if one can call, then why visit?

REFLECTIONS ON COMMUNITY

What kind of modern communication—despite its benefits—do you find intrudes on family life? What can you do to safeguard significant times, such as during meals?

This week, practice the art of a face-to-face visit. Make a list of people you'd like to visit with and get started.

Try stopping to talk with neighbors when you're out for a walk.

When others come to your door, practice your own hospitality—get in the habit of inviting them in, instead of conducting your business at the door. What are some other ways your home could be even more inviting to guests?

PLAIN *Living*

Women in a family get together for workdays once a month. The mother and her grown daughters and daughters-in-law will take turns meeting at each other's home to help with cleaning, baking, canning, sewing, or quilting.[11]

For the Good of the Community

If you are true to your faith, there are things you give up for your faith.

Amish Proverb

A young Amish man thought about starting a furniture-building shop. His bishop advised him that, instead, their area could really use another buggy shop. This young man had all kinds of skills: farming and dairying, metal work and woodwork, but he didn't know how to build a buggy. For the greater good of the community, this young man set aside his own desire and agreed to start a buggy shop. First, though, he needed to learn the craft of buggy building.

So he went to work for the owner of the only other buggy shop in the community. The owner of that buggy shop knew of the young man's intent to start his own shop one day. On the very first day, the buggy builder told the young man that he would be treated like he was a son. He taught the young man the craft of buggy making, including his bookkeeping system, where to find the best products at the most competitive prices, and all of his trade secrets. For the greater good of the community, the experienced buggy builder held nothing back, fully aware that he was helping to create competition for himself.

Today, the young man has a thriving buggy shop. His wife works with him, sewing the upholstered cushions that fit the foam seats. They estimate that only about 40 percent of the business is for new buggies; the other 60 percent is for repairs and maintenance. The bishop was right—there was a need for another buggy shop. By setting such a selfless, noncompetitive example, the experienced buggy builder only hoped that others would do the same, when they had the chance.

Cooperation is a cornerstone for the Amish way of life. It is a value that is ingrained at home, reinforced in school, and illustrated in the community. As cooperation is encouraged, competition is equally discouraged. Even on the playground.

Matthew is a thirteen-year-old Amish boy who loves softball. Maybe a little too much, worries his teacher. "Just the other day," said Lydia, Matthew's grandmother, "Matthew told us that he was playing softball during recess and yelled to his team to get some hits. He was frustrated because his team was losing. The teacher chided him. Said he shouldn't be so concerned about winning."

The problem with winning is . . . it requires someone to lose.

Comparisons, like competition, are discouraged by the Amish. For example, an Amish teacher would never grade on a curve. Doing so would mean that one child's good grade depends on another child's poor grade. The children encourage one another's good performance so that the whole class or school may do well. Differences in learning are acknowledged and respected by the teacher and the children. "Hard learners probably have an easier time of it here than if they were in the public education," said Susie, mother of six. "They're still 'in the conversation.'" She means that an individual is valued, even if he learns at a slower pace and can't keep up with his peers. To the Amish point of view, there is a place and a purpose for each person, like pieces of a pie. Each person is part of the whole.

The very nature of competition seeks to extol an individual by crowding out rivals, causing them to fail. To lose. In the upside-down world of the Amish, they seek to build community by helping all individuals succeed. Everyone wins.

REFLECTIONS ON COMMUNITY

If you decided that community came first, what would you do differently?

It is easy to criticize and exclude a person who is weak or immature. What is God's perspective about such individuals?

The need to feel superior to another often goes hand in hand with competitiveness. Is there someone within your family or church whom you have been tempted to criticize instead of love?

What are some ways you can reduce competition and comparisons at home and increase acceptance for each family member? Start recognizing comparisons as peace thieves.

PLAIN *Living*

The Amish consider that the sin of *Hochmut*, a word that connotes arrogance and haughtiness as well as pride, is among the worst, the root of many other sins. The Ordnung is designed to prevent the members from falling prey to sins such as Hochmut.[12]

Amish Quilts

If you sense your faith is unraveling, go back to where you dropped the thread of obedience.

Amish Proverb

I f you think of an Old Order Amish grandmother as a plain-faced, plain-spoken woman, like Marilla Cuthbert in *Anne of Green Gables*, Leanne Miller comes as a surprise. A warm smile etched on her face, Leanne is a quick moving woman, quick in thought, word, and deed. And she knows how to manage a successful business.

As tourists walk into the dimly lit basement of Leanne's shop, they stop to catch their breath, giving their eyes time to adjust to the vibrant colors. Then the oohs and aahs start winding up, like a siren. Museum-quality quilts are everywhere, neatly hung in racks against the walls or piled on a bed in the center of the basement.

With one hand, Leanne directs a customer to a quilt folded under a table. With the other hand, she holds two light-colored pillows against the window, peering carefully to discern the shades. "That's the one," she decides confidently. "That's the one that will match the quilt you bought. It will draw out the colors of the background."

Clearly, Leanne has a keen eye for color. She learned to quilt from her mother. She and her husband, Paul, have four daughters and five sons, and many grandchildren. As her daughters grew, Leanne taught them how to piece, stencil, and quilt different patterns.

One day, a traveling salesman dropped by Leanne and Paul's farm, noticed her fine quilts, and suggested that she try to sell them. With a little help from her mother-in-law, Leanne opened up a quilt shop on the farm to earn extra money for the family. Just thirty minutes after she hung her quilt shop sign for the first time, a customer arrived at her door.

"Quilts were a part of my life for about as long as I can remember," says Emily, one of Leanne's daughters. "I still remember that feeling of excitement of getting our first customer after we put out our little homemade sign. I was only about eight years old at the time, so it was not until several years later that I actually started helping to make quilts and wait on customers in the quilt shop."

Leanne chooses the colors and orders the fabrics, then sends the pieces out to the Amish women who have become part of her cottage industry network. "I have hundreds of women working for me," she says. Leanne has very high standards for her quilters. Each quilt has tiny, even stitches. They range in price from $400 to thousands of dollars, especially for "white-on-white." Each is hand-stitched with loving care and signed by the quilter.

Quilting is an important part of the social life of Amish women. A quilting "bee" or "frolic" is organized by a woman who has a finished quilt top, ready to be quilted. The host invites her guests— often sisters or cousins—and provides the noon meal. A group of experienced quilters can finish a quilt in a day. If a woman were to quilt the top alone, it would take weeks of steady work. These gatherings, like a barn raising or haymaking, weave together the pleasures of friendship and community with the principles of work and mutual support—so essential to the Amish culture.

"Quilting bees are a big part of our community," adds Emily. "Though the quilts we make to sell are usually stitched by one person or a mother and her daughters, the quilts we make for our own use are more often quilted at a quilting bee. My friends and our mothers would get together several times a year and quilt a quilt for one of the girls or sometimes for another sibling. It was always a lot of fun, and there was always a lot of good food!"

Following World War II, quiltmaking was virtually abandoned by most American women, considered to be too old-fashioned and time consuming. Not so for the Amish. Quilting has remained an integral part of Amish life. Despite their small numbers and humble lifestyle, the contribution of Amish women to the art of American quiltmaking has been unique and far-reaching.

The Amish would frown at the idea of their quilts being called an "art form." They would say that their quiltmaking only embodies all they hold dear. Their quilts are like their community—simple, strong, purposeful, and serene.

Reflections on Community

What kinds of traditions do you have in your family or circle of friends? How do those traditions draw you together? Commit to keeping those traditions alive. Don't let busyness crowd out those important, relationship-affirming activities.

What are some new ways to create neighborliness in your church community or neighborhood?

Have you discovered the joy of working with your hands to create something beautiful? Gardening, cooking, sewing, knitting, carpentry—all can bring connections to other people and a deep inner satisfaction.

PLAIN *Living*

Amish women sew by hand and with a machine that is operated by a foot pedal. Payment is based on the number of yards of thread used. The spools of thread are 250 yards long, so the bill for the work is usually toted up when a spool is exhausted. According to a quilt shop owner, it takes about four weeks of full-time work to complete a large quilt.[13]

Growing Up Amish

Put the swing where the children want it. The grass will grow back.

Amish Proverb

Bena Byler shaded her eyes against the setting sun and scanned the yard for her daughter. "Malinda! Malinda!"

Seven-year-old Malinda heard her mother's voice calling to her and knew she was in trouble. She'd been playing with her sisters down by the stream and lost track of time. Barefooted, she ran like lightning to the large white dairy barn, flying past her mother standing at the kitchen door. She slid open the heavy barn door with a rumble, releasing the warm, musty air. She hoped her father was busy in the back.

Alas. Arms crossed, eyebrows raised, her father leaned against the doorjamb. He pointed to a bucket that held an enormous baby bottle, filled with fresh milk. He clucked his tongue. "That calf is mighty hungry, Mindy. He's been bawling."

Avoiding his eyes, Malinda whispered an apology, took the bottle, tucked it under her arm, and hurried to the stall where the calf was crying out. She unlocked the door and hopped down into the hay-filled stall. Skillfully, she grabbed the newborn calf around the neck and thrust the nipple into his mouth. The hungry beast quickly caught on and started to gulp milk, freshly delivered from the herd, his first meal from his mother's milk supply.

Malinda's parents, Bena and John Fisher, run a dairy of forty-nine cows, large even by Amish standards. The dairy takes up every spare minute of their day, especially in springtime when the heifers go fresh—which, in farmerspeak, means they deliver calves.

Bena and John count on help from their children—all seven of them, four girls and three boys. It's Malinda's job to bottle feed the newborns. Nine-year-old Sarah cares for the chickens. Eight-year-old Elsie hoes the garden. Five-year-old John Junior sweeps the kitchen floor. Even three-year-old Becky takes her mother's notes out to the barn to deliver to her father.

At a young age, Amish children are expected to be "choring," meaning they are given tasks to complete around the house and farm. Most of us would be amazed to observe the level of responsibility that Amish children are given on a farm, and their responsibilities increase with their age. Four- and five-year-olds pump water by hand, learn how to milk cows, and do other farm-related chores.

Amish boys do the work of a man by the time they're eight. "When I was just six or seven," said John, "I was doing field work with horses. My father put me on a two-horse manure spreader on a cold winter day when the ground was still frozen. It wasn't muddy yet so the horses could walk easily, and it would give the manure time to age on the fields. I could manage the team down a row, but I hadn't learned how to turn the horses around at the end of the field and head them back the other direction. I'd yell to my older brother, who was working in the barn. He would run to me over the crusty earth and turn my horses around so I could head back up the other way. Slow going, but I learned."

The Amish believe that a farm is the best place to raise children. Life around the farm provides many opportunities for teaching children foundational values: daily lessons in mutual dependency. The animals depend on them as they depend on the animals, the children depend on their parents as the parents depend on the children for help. The family depends on their community for aid and for social interaction. Their community, individuals who make up a whole, ultimately depends on God—his gifts of rain and sun to grow the crops. The farm is a living classroom, symbolizing all that is good in the Amish life.

Bena is over in the garden with John Junior, arms wrapped around him, holding a hoe, pushing the soil without uprooting young plants. Another slow process, but John Junior is learning how to do the task properly. "It's our job to train our children for life, and life requires work," Bena explains. "But we don't see work as a bad thing. We see it as a gift from God."

John Junior takes the hoe from her and tries to do a row on his own. Bena smiles, pleased at his initiative. "Besides," she says, eyes crinkling at the corners, "hard work never hurt anybody."

REFLECTIONS ON COMMUNITY

What kinds of skills did you learn from your parents? Cooking? Gardening? Carpentry? Are you passing those on to your children?

Modern American children—and their parents—live jam-packed lives. Because of busy schedules, it is easy to justify not requiring our children to help around the house. Sometimes it's easier just to do a chore ourselves. But do you ever wonder if you ask enough of your children? Consider handing over at least one age-appropriate responsibility: set the table or wash the car. It takes effort, but the payoff can last a lifetime.

PLAIN *Living*

After children leave school at eighth grade and begin working, they often give their paychecks to their parents until they marry or turn twenty-one. The parents will give them a small allowance and bank the remainder until the child marries, when most parents help with the purchase of land, a house and/or starting a business.[14]

The Burning Barn

A farm is not a farm without its barn.

Amish Proverb

One autumn day, newlyweds Aaron and Rachel King moved onto a sixty-acre dairy farm in a small rural town in Pennsylvania, a wedding gift from Aaron's father. The two-story white frame house sat tucked against the hill, the dairy barn below it, close to the road. From the kitchen window, Rachel could watch Aaron at work.

One late summer afternoon, Aaron was burning debris on a hill behind the barn. It was nearly dark when he realized that an ember from the fire had blown downwind into the barn—a barn filled with recently harvested hay. Dry hay. By the time the fire department arrived—most of them family members, Amish neighbors, and friends—the barn had burned completely to the ground. Two horses, trapped in their stalls, died in the fire, but Aaron's herd of dairy cows was safe. They were still out in the pasture, waiting to be brought in for the evening milking.

Typical of the Amish, Aaron and Rachel quickly moved past the shock of the event to problem solving. Fire or no fire, forty-two cows still needed to be milked. Aaron remembered that a neighbor's farm was up for sale, vacant, but the milking equipment was still on site. Thinking quickly, Aaron was able to move his cows with their swollen udders from the pasture and guide them across the road, right into the neighbor's empty barn. Those wide-eyed cows didn't even realize all that had happened between the morning milking and the evening milking.

Early the next day, neighbors of Aaron and Rachel arrived, unasked but expected, to help clear away the debris. Walking around the barn's empty footprint, the men told Aaron that they were grateful the barn was entirely gone. "We'll waste no time in trying to salvage what remains," one fellow said, stroking his long whiskers. Within the hour, another neighbor arrived, bringing a tractor with steel tires to carry away and bury the horses' carcasses. Before lunch, the Amish barn builder and his crew arrived, ready to draw up plans for the new barn. The materials were ordered that very day.

Most of the components of the barn were prepared in advance so that the heavy lifting could be done when workers were present. All the timbers that made up the frame of the barn were joined by wooden pins inserted into holes where the two timbers were joined. The timbers, eight to ten inches on each side, were pre-cut and notched and joined together on the ground before the day of the barn raising.

Aaron and Rachel would be responsible for about 25 percent of the cost of their new barn. The Amish Aid Society, headquartered in Pennsylvania, would cover the remaining 75 percent. All of the labor and food provided was free, a gift of time and resources to a neighbor in need. "This way," explained the barn builder, "there is something of everybody in the barn."

The barn builder set the date for raising Aaron and Rachel's new barn. Neighbors knew about the event by word of mouth; the date was announced at nearby churches. Women in their church organized meals for two hundred workers who were expected.

On the set Saturday, workers arrived at Aaron and Rachel's farm by dawn. An observer would have had trouble discerning who was supervising the barn raising. Everyone had a job to do. All able-bodied men and teenagers pitched in; older men directed, young boys acted as gofers and hunted the ground for fallen nails. Women and girls prepared the noon meal: hearty food to keep the workers well fortified. Meat loaf and noodles, potatoes, gravy, chow-chow, pickled beets, gelatin salads, pies, and cookies.

Late in the morning, a deep, authoritative voice rang out: *"Faerdich?"* The women, girls, and boys dropped what they were doing. All eyes were on the barn site. Dozens of men grabbed hold of ropes to hoist the assembled ends and sides of the barn, carefully raising its frame into place.

Climbing with great agility, the men shimmied up the bones of the barn. Covering the roof as thick as bees, the men pounded out a symphony of nails with every shingle.

By dusk, Aaron and Rachel's barn was nearly complete. Big, solid, rectangular, with siding of narrow, freshly sawn boards that shone pale yellow against the setting sun. *"Gutgemacht!"* shouted the barn builder, signaling the day's end. (Well-done!) Interior finish work remained for Aaron to fill his spare time this winter, but the barn was snug, watertight. It was even filled with hay, provided by neighbors, to replace what had been lost to the fire. The cows were in their new stanchions, ready for the evening milking.

Just two weeks after the fire.

Reflections on Community

A burning barn is a very visual need. Neighbors could see the trouble Aaron and Rachel were in. They knew what needed to be done, and they went to work. Consider a burning barn as a metaphor for a genuine need. Is there a "burning barn" near you? Or even a smoldering ember? Help meet that need today.

Often, it is easier to give help than to receive it. Aaron and Rachel were willing to accept help from their community. What do you need help with?

Besides the obvious, practical benefit of a new barn, what intangible benefits did the community provide to Aaron and Rachel? How could you apply that to the community you live in?

PLAIN *Living*

The location and placing of the barn in relation to the house and rest of the farm is considered. House and barn usually stand at right angles to each other, with a southern exposure preferable for the house. To create natural drainage, the barn usually stands on an incline in the contour of the landscape.[15]

Part 4

Forgiveness

We should not put a question mark where God puts a period.

Amish Proverb

Deborah is a soft-spoken eighteen-year-old Amish woman who lives at home and works in her mother's quilt shop. On her feet are bright orange crocs; a bandanna is fastened around her hair with hot pink hair clips. She's never heard of iPods or of Lindsay Lohan's travails. But she radiates a calm maturity that outshines any typical teenager.

One of Deborah's older sisters moved to a nearby farm when she married. Her four children, Deborah's nieces and nephew, attended a one-room schoolhouse—the West Nickel Mines School. The school was one of ten Amish schools in the West Nickel Mines (Bart Township) community. Amish parochial schools are small, often one room, snugly tucked in the corner of a farmer's land, close enough for neighborhood children to trek alongside the country roads. An average classroom holds twenty-five to thirty students. Many of the children are related to each other; if not siblings, they might be cousins.

On October 2, 2006, a deranged man—a milk truck driver with a childhood grudge—burst into the West Nickel Mines School with guns. He sent the boys out of the school and held the girls as hostages. Forty-five minutes later, he shot ten little girls before turning the gun on himself. Three girls died instantly, one of whom was Deborah's niece. Another niece, still alive, was airlifted to a hospital, fighting for her life. A third niece miraculously escaped. "She ran out of the door when she heard a woman's voice tell her,

'If you want to leave, go quietly.' But no one was nearby to say that to her." Deborah paused, adding shyly, "We think it was an angel who told her to go."

The teacher had escaped, and the adults had been ordered by the gunman to leave the schoolhouse, along with the boys—one of whom was Deborah's nephew. Deborah's niece who was shot and seriously wounded did survive, though she has required extensive surgeries to rebuild her shoulder socket. "It's a miracle, really," Deborah said, her bright brown eyes shining. "She's doing so well. It's healing so she'll be completely normal."

It occurred to me that four of Deborah's family members were in that schoolroom. Four! And yet she spoke without pity. In fact, she didn't sound bitter about the senseless tragedy. "We just have to keep going on," she said, in a soft, matter-of-fact tone. But she was quick to point out that it hasn't been easy. "It was really tough. We did question 'why?' We wondered why God let this happen. People think we're perfect, but we're not. Yet we can't *dwell* on what happened. We have to leave it in God's hands."

In the book *Amish Grace*, author Donald B. Kraybill noted that of all the interviews he conducted after the West Nickel Mines tragedy, he never heard an Amish person doubt the existence of a loving God. They believe that God is with them *through* such a horrific event. And they have a deep and abiding hope in eternal life.

But what shocked the world was the Amish of West Nickel Mines' powerful example of forgiveness extended to the gunman and his family. More than half of those who attended the driver's funeral were Amish. His widow was invited to the Amish children's funerals. As money and gifts poured in, the Amish included the widow and her children in distribution of the gifts.

Forgiveness can be achingly difficult. It is an unnatural act for our very flawed human natures. Yet the Amish seem to have a better grasp on authentic forgiveness than many of us. *Demut*—humility—is a deeply rooted value for the Amish. They know they are sinners, dependent on God's grace. The Amish read from one text, the Bible. "For if you forgive men when they sin against you, your heavenly Father will also forgive you. But if you do not forgive men their sins, your Father will not forgive your sins" (Matt. 6:14–15). They take those verses literally. In them, Jesus did not mention whether a sinner seeks forgiveness; he only mentioned a person's obligation to forgive. Put that way, if the Amish can't forgive others, how can they possibly expect God to forgive them?

By God's grace, I hope none of us will ever need to forgive someone for a crime against our loved ones like the shootings at West Nickel Mines School. Yet I believe we can work on letting go of hurts, both large and small. We can improve our forgiving skills, believing, as the Amish do, that feelings follow intention. We can seek to forgive others, as the Father has forgiven us.

Trusting in God, recounting the good things, not dwelling on tragedy, a firm belief in heaven, and extending forgiveness—these were the tools the Amish used to cope and heal from the wound of that event. As Deborah repeated, "We just have to keep going on with life."

The way she said it, so strong and sure, sounded like a benediction.

The Freedom of Forgiveness

A heart touched by grace brings joy to the face.

Amish Proverb

On a typical autumn Sunday morning, Beth Kime confided to a friend at church that she was worried her seventeen-year-old son, Joel, had been driving too fast. Like most teenaged boys, he had a fondness for speeding. "Maybe we should take his license away for a month," Beth told her friend.

A few hours later, Joel was driving to a local school for an afternoon game of football. In the car were his younger brother, Jeff, and two friends, Chad and Dave. "I saw an Amish buggy about a hundred yards in front of us in our lane, heading the same direction as us," Joel remembered. "I said to everyone in the car something like, 'I'm going to blow by these guys.'"

As Joel overtook the buggy, he didn't see the buggy's left turn signal or the small country road the buggy was turning into. "I will never, ever forget seeing the nose of the horse turn out in front of me," he said. The car smashed into the buggy. The buggy flew over the top of Joel's car. Everyone in Joel's car was relatively unharmed, but an Amish man climbed out of the shattered buggy, yelling frantically, "Does anyone know CPR?"

The man's wife was fatally injured in the crash. The couple were on their honeymoon, Amish style, going from relative to relative. They had only been married for five days. Aaron, the groom, was twenty-one years old. Sarah, his bride, was nineteen.

The next day, Joel's parents insisted that he visit the Amish family and attend the viewing. "I felt so nervous, there was actually pain ripping across my guts," Joel said. Joel had grown up in Lancaster County but admitted he hadn't paid much attention to the Amish subculture that surrounded him. "I didn't know what these people were like or what was going to happen. Would they come pouring out of the porch with shotguns?"

When Joel's family arrived at the viewing, buggies were parked all over the farm property, heightening his fear. The family knew he was coming and met them in the front room. Sarah's parents, Melvin and Barbara, walked up to him and put their arms around him. "Through tears I muttered how sorry I was, and they spoke the most incredible words that were possible to utter: 'We forgive you; we know it was God's time for her to die.' "

Aaron, like Sarah's parents, came to Joel with open arms.

"He simply forgave me. We hugged as the freedom of forgiveness swept over and through me." Joel could not express the relief that flooded over him. "Their initial forgiveness was so meaningful, so powerful, that as early as the next day, it had changed everything for me. The slate was wiped clean, once and for all."

The authentic forgiveness extended by the Amish family went even further. They befriended Joel and his family, inviting them over for dinner. They wrote letters to the judge to beg for a pardon of the charges. (Joel was a minor, so was able to avoid serving a prison sentence, but he did lose his driver's license for three years, paid fines, and was required to serve 200 hours of community service.) When Joel was married, they attended his wedding. And when he and his wife went on the mission field to Jamaica, they supported him financially.

"I often think of that day," Joel said. "I drive by the accident site almost every week. I still wish it would never have happened."

Beth, Joel's mother, wished "hundreds of times" that she had taken Joel's license away from him at church that Sunday. "Sarah would still be alive!"

But they are quick to say that out of the tragedy came a blessing. "They had forgiven me, and they never, ever went back on that decision," reflected Joel. "And they backed it up with a real relationship. It was powerful. It was consuming."

Since that time, Joel said he has never had trouble forgiving people. "I think God must have changed my heart, because I don't have to try to forgive anymore. It flows out as naturally as my heart beats without me having a say in the matter."

For Joel, the Amish family's ready forgiveness repeats itself over and over.

REFLECTIONS ON FORGIVENESS

Joel came to Aaron the next day after the accident, seeking forgiveness. How do you think you would have responded if you had been in Aaron's position?

Later, Joel's family learned that coming to the viewing and accepting responsibility for the tragedy was a necessary step for the Amish family to heal. The family told Joel's mother, Beth, "When you came to us, our healing began." Pray for the courage to face those you've hurt, knowing that it leads to peace.

God doesn't ask us to forgive others because it's the right or moral thing to do. He asks us to forgive others on the basis of a foundational truth—his great love for us.

PLAIN *Living*

There are more than fourteen hundred Old Order Amish church districts, and each is more or less independent, with its own Ordnung.[1]

When Forgiveness Doesn't Happen

The person who forgives does more for himself than for anyone else.

Amish Proverb

Years later, a member of the church that Joel Kime attended experienced the opposite of Joel's story. The gentleman was returning home from work one evening. He fell asleep at the wheel and smashed into an Amish horse and buggy. Inside the buggy were an Amish couple and two English children whom the couple were babysitting. The Amish couple survived, but later that night, the two children died of injuries sustained in the accident.

The man who caused the accident took full responsibility for his mistake. He was a broken man. He literally threw himself at the feet of the English parents, begging for forgiveness. He was turned away. "The father was especially cold," Joel said. "He even threatened the man and his family." The father of those children could not and would not forgive him.

"No matter what the man did, expressing how sorry he was for causing the accident, the father could not get over it," Joel said. The English mother was able to extend some forgiveness to him. "But a hardness of heart ate away at the soul of the father. It resulted in him leaving his wife. Eventually, he committed suicide, leaving everyone with unresolved guilt."

In contrast to his own experience with being forgiven, Joel realized that the parishioner was never set free. "He longed for the freedom of forgiveness I received, but was instead locked in a prison of guilt."

Even more tragic, Joel said, was that the English father was chained into a prison worse than that of the man who caused the accident. "A prison of hatred and mistrust that ultimately led him to no other option of dealing with the pain than to take his own life."

The Amish family who lost their daughter during Joel's accident handled the tragedy in an entirely different way. "They coped in the months and years afterward by ministering to other Amish and English families who had been dealt a blow of tragic losses of loved ones," Joel said.

Forgiveness, Joel said, is a practical application of a decision to trust God with one's life. "To forgive is to trust that he will take care of us. To not forgive is to say to him that I will handle this. To forgive is to release the captive into God's care. To not forgive is to chain that captive into a prison of guilt."

The Lord's Prayer in Matthew 6 and the two verses that follow it are central to Amish worship, life, and faith—holding great spiritual and social significance. They believe there are some strings attached to God's grace and forgiveness: to pass on the forgiveness to others. Joel's life testifies to the power of that belief—he is now a pastor in Lancaster, Pennsylvania.

That choice, the Amish believe, holds eternal consequences.

Reflections on Forgiveness

We all have events that are difficult to forgive. Write down one today and visualize yourself handing it over to God, trusting that he will take care of it for you.

Humility, says Jesus, is not only a condition of greatness, but essential for entering God's kingdom (Matt. 18:3–4).

Think of people you've known who have chosen not to forgive but instead have held a grudge for months or even years. How would you characterize them?

Sometimes conflicts tempt us to discouragement and despair. How would viewing the conflict as an opportunity for Christ to live in us change your perspective?

PLAIN *Living*

In preliminary results of a study called the Stanford Forgiveness Project, a researcher found that those who forgave others reduced stress symptoms such as headaches, stomachaches, dizziness, fatigue, and muscle aches.[2]

The Comfort Quilt

Good deeds have echoes.

Amish Proverb

One month after the 9/11 terrorist attacks on the World Trade Center in New York City, students from St. Hilary Catholic School in Fairlawn, Ohio, created a quilt for students at St. James Catholic School in New Jersey. A number of St. James schoolchildren had lost parents, relatives, and neighbors in the attacks. The children of St. Hilary made the quilt as a way to let those grieving children know that others cared about their loss and shared their sorrow. The patches of the quilt were colored by the children with happy images of hearts and rainbows. Named the "Comfort Quilt," it was hung in the halls of St. James.

Four years later, Hurricane Katrina hit the Gulf Coast, devastating a wide area. It quickly gained the distinction of being the worst natural disaster that the United States had ever experienced. The St. James Catholic School in New Jersey decided to forward the Comfort Quilt to the St. Joseph Catholic School in Madison, Mississippi. St. Joseph's had taken in over 125 students who had been forced to evacuate from the hurricane because they lost their homes. And there the Comfort Quilt found a new home.

In October of 2006, one year after Hurricane Katrina, the children from the St. Joseph school knew their quilt needed to provide comfort to another group of children. The quilt was sent to the Old Order Amish community in West Nickel Mines, Pennsylvania, after the one-room Amish schoolhouse shootings, in which a man killed five girls and injured five others. The children of St. James wanted the Amish families of West Nickel Mines to know they offered their support, prayers, and comfort. The quilt was hung in Bart Township Fire Station 51, the station that acted as first responders to the shootings and became the hub of community care for that emotionally wrenching week.

Everyone hoped the Comfort Quilt would remain at Bart Township Fire Station 51. If it were sent elsewhere, it would mean that another major tragedy had occurred that had affected innocent children.

Six months later, that's just what happened.

On April 16, 2007, a student of Virginia Tech went on a campus shooting rampage that took the lives of thirty-two faculty and students.

Later that summer, representatives from each Amish family—forty people—who were affected by the West Nickel Mines shootings traveled by bus to Blacksburg, Virginia. They wanted to personally deliver the Comfort Quilt to Virginia Tech. It was carried in a wooden box made by a member of their community, along with a framed history of the quilt and a painted picture of the schoolhouse. A letter accompanied the quilt from the West Nickel Mines community, expressing that they "have felt the same emotions of disbelief, a sense of helplessness, anger, despair, and depression . . . [they] understand."

"It is unfortunate that tragedy connected our two communities," said Dr. John E. Dooley, vice president for outreach and international affairs at Virginia Tech, "but we will forever cherish a special bond and friendship with the Amish families of Nickel Mines.

They brought to our community a strong message of condolence, support, and forgiveness."

The university hosted a special lunch for the Amish representatives on campus and invited the families of local victims—two faculty members and a freshman student. "I was initially struck by the contrasts of innovation and technology and the simplicity of our guests," noted Dooley. "Nevertheless, the bond between us was instant and strong."

Then Dooley took the families to the memorial to the slain victims on the drill field. "The Amish inspected each and every stone. They already knew the names. I was moved."

As they presented the university with the Comfort Quilt, the Amish said that since the quilt was now in Virginia Tech's possession, it would be the school's responsibility to pass it along in the event of a tragedy elsewhere. But they added that they hoped that the quilt would stay at Virginia Tech and gather dust.

Sadly, the Comfort Quilt has since been moved to Northern Illinois University, to comfort the victims of yet another school shooting rampage.

"But it was here," Dooley said. "It hung in our campus War Memorial Chapel, where it brought comfort and peace." He paused. "There was indeed comfort."

REFLECTIONS ON FORGIVENESS

The Amish were able to offer comfort to the Virginia Tech community because they had experienced a similar event. Consider your difficulties—how can you reach out to help others in similar situations?

The Amish visitors honored the losses at Virginia Tech by learning the names of every single victim. Don't be afraid to talk to a grieving person or to bring up the name of the one they are grieving over—it's often what they most need.

Does this story change how you might work through grief or a sad experience with your child?

How have you been comforted in a time of grief? What was the most effective means others used to comfort you?

PLAIN *Living*

One book that is kept in nearly every Amish home and school is *Martyrs' Mirror*, a book of more than twelve hundred pages, originally compiled between 1562 and 1685, though the version most used today is the one put together by Thieleman J. Van Braght of Holland in 1660. It consists of accounts of martyrdoms of various Christian faithful from the time of Jesus onward. The book evolved during the era when Anabaptists were being imprisoned, tortured, and executed for their faith, and its original intent was to instruct Anabaptists on what actions to take and what to say in response to interrogators' questions when their expected turns on the rack arrived.[3]

A Sacred Silence

Blessed are they who have nothing to say, and who cannot be persuaded to say it.

Amish Proverb

I t is Sunday. As the clock strikes eight in the morning, Amish families pour out of their homes and start up the steep hill to the home where church will be held today. They walk in groups of two or three, side by side, with children straggling behind. For the most part, they walk without talking. A few come in buggies, but the hill is steep and families have to get out and lighten the load for the horse. Even still, words are few. Silence descends once more, silence and the sweet sense of waiting.

The worship service begins with silence. There's a distinct orderliness to the way people flow in to their seats. First the ordained men, then the rest of the men, in order of age. Then women, girls, and young children file in, wordlessly, shake hands with the ministers, and sit on the opposite side. The boys follow. Between hymns there are long periods of silence. The whole assembly kneels for silent prayer; the prayer ends with a clearing of the throat by the minister. Silent prayer during the church service draws the community into humility and bareness before God.

"It is only in silence that we can hear Christ," says Ruby Zook, a small, compact woman with graying hair tucked beneath her prayer cap. When she smiles, which is often, it seems like the sun washes over her skin. She folds her hands in front of her stomach, outer evidence of inner calm. "When we fail to practice silence, God must go to great lengths to get our attention through all the noisiness of our own thoughts, the noisiness of our feelings, the noisiness of the world."

Ruby believes that there are times when people need to be quiet to ponder the meaning and savor the communion with God. "Don't you think that Peter, James, and John were quiet as they hiked with the Lord Jesus up the mountain for the transfiguration? They knew something special was about to happen," she says. "And I'm sure they were quiet again as they came back down, filled up with that experience. Words would have failed them."

The Amish value humility and meekness, often to the point of speaking softly and slowly. Sermons emphasize biblical warnings that "everyone should be . . . slow to speak" (James 1:19). To the Amish, humility, known as Demut, goes hand in hand with silence.

At the family table, silent prayers bookend each meal with reverence, offered both before and after. The head of the household clears his throat or gives a brief nod of his head to signal the prayer is over. Conversation for its own sake is not encouraged. "Though some families are naturally quiet," explains Ruby, "and some are naturally talkative."

On Sunday an attitude of reverence prevails. Sundays at home are spent without the usual workday sounds—hammering, building, or boisterous noises are prohibited, even whistling. Relaxed conversation, resting, and walking are silences that blend with attitudes of worship. When a church member confesses a sin before the church, all is forgiven; the slate is wiped cleaned as if it never happened. The sin is never spoken of again. Silence becomes restorative. If cursed or mocked by an outsider, the Amish person answers with silence. This is his way of turning the other cheek, of expressing pacifistic beliefs that reach back to the martyrs and to Christ himself, who refused to answer the questions of Pontius Pilate.

"There is no substitute for silence," adds Ruby. "No trick. No shortcut. In our selfishness we can imagine that we give God the gift of our time in silence, that we are offering something at his altar. We have it backwards. He gives us the gift of his wisdom, but it is only available if we can silence our noisy selves, the noisy world, and find him and his wisdom within. It isn't a question of being comfortable with silence. Silence is not about comfort. It is about obedience."

Silence emphasizes what you do over what you say. Silence is not the absence of communication but a powerful expression of it. Sympathy and understanding, for the Amish, come in the form of a Sunday afternoon visit. Love comes with a look of satisfaction over the heads of the children at the kitchen table. Help is not offered in words—it is simply given.

REFLECTIONS ON FORGIVENESS

By nature some of us are more verbal than others. Some are more reserved. When is silence not golden?

Most likely, today will provide plenty of opportunities to say something that shouldn't be said. Hold back from speaking. Instead, seek to understand another's point of view.

When the Amish attend a viewing before a funeral, they do not talk to each other. Their sympathy is implied with their presence. It's an example in which nonverbal communication might be more powerful than verbal communication. Today, say who you are with actions instead of words.

When have you experienced the need or desire for sacred silence? How would talking have changed the mood?

How can you create more room for silence in your life? Or become more comfortable with silence?

PLAIN *Living*

There is an absence of courtesy words in Amish speech. With outsiders, they will accommodate the requirement for polite language, but among themselves, in their own language, they rarely use "pardon me" or "excuse me." It's a practice that dates back to medieval Europe, as the Amish became a distinct group. In those days, courtesy words were characteristic of the nobility, considered meaningless and excessive.

The Slingshot

There are no degrees of honesty.

Amish Proverb

O n a muggy summer Sunday afternoon with a sky as gray as a flannel blanket, six-year-old Tobe Miller was informed by his mother that they were going to visit cousin Miriam. Tobe's father and older brothers stayed behind to take care of the evening milking. "*Mach schnell*, Tobe," said his mother, reaching a hand down to hoist him into the buggy. *Hurry up.* "I want to get there and back before the rain hits."

Tobe peered at the dense clouds that squatted heavy on the valley, compressing the air, as the buggy horse lunged forward. He enjoyed visits at Miriam's farm. Joe, Miriam's son, was just a few years older than he was. Tobe was the caboose in his family, so to have a built-in playmate was his idea of a perfect summer afternoon. He just hoped the rain would hold off.

As soon as they arrived, Tobe hurried to the barn to find Joe. The two boys slid down haystacks with their arms folded across their chests. After the haystacks, they tried to snag a fish or two down by the pond. Then, making sure their mothers weren't within eyeshot or earshot, they tried to put a harness on the billy goat. An angry goat wasn't as much fun as they had hoped, so they quickly abandoned that idea. Soon, they grew bored.

Joe decided that he'd rather go hunt cottontails with his new slingshot than sit around. His mother had been after him to whittle down the rabbit population that helped itself to her garden. Distracted by the plump raspberries that lined his mother's garden, Joe let Tobe try out the slingshot while he filled his cheeks with berries. Tobe was enamored with the slingshot. He didn't hit any cottontails like Joe did, but he knew he could, with more practice.

Too soon, Joe's mother rang the triangle iron bell, signaling that it was time to milk the cows. Joe raced to the barn, forgetting Tobe. Forgetting the slingshot. Tobe looked at the slingshot, rubbed his fingers along the smooth wood, and made a spur-of-the-moment decision. He tucked the slingshot into the back of his pants and covered the pants with his coat.

After Tobe and his mother returned home, he jumped off the buggy to help unhitch the horse. As he reached up to get the bridle off of the horse's forehead, his coat pulled up. His mother caught sight of the slingshot tucked in his waist. She yanked it out and held it up. "What's this, Tobe?"

Tobe's cheeks flamed. "Oh. That. It must be Joe's. Guess I forgot to give it back to him."

His mother looked him straight in the eye. She knew, in that uncanny ability that mothers seem to have, that he was lying. Without another word, she put the bridle back on the weary horse and told Tobe to climb in the buggy. "We're going back."

"Now?" Tobe asked in a shaky voice, dread rising.

Like most Plain women, Tobe's mother rarely showed much emotion on her face, but at that moment there was fire in her eyes and color in her cheeks. "Now. You are going to apologize to Joe, return the slingshot, and ask him to forgive you."

As if on cue, the drizzling rain that had begun on the way home thickened to a leaden downpour. Even the horse gave Tobe a dark look.

Fifty-four years later, Tobe remembered every detail of that afternoon as if it were yesterday. What stood out in his mind was the part about asking for forgiveness. Joe readily forgave him, and things were patched up between them. Tobe and Joe have remained close throughout their lives. The slingshot thievery was never spoken of again.

REFLECTIONS ON FORGIVENESS

Sin destroys peace, and when we lose our peace, sin is often present. Don't ignore or deny it—ask for God's help to identify sin (a definite act of disobedience) that has broken your peace.

According to 1 John 1:9, "If we confess our sins, he is faithful and just and will forgive us our sins and purify us from all unrighteousness." This is how we restore peace with God.

No relationship is without conflict. It isn't easy to ask for forgiveness when you realize you've been in the wrong. And it isn't easy to forgive someone when they've hurt you deeply. And yet, forgiveness is a necessary ingredient in restoring relationships. If someone asks for your forgiveness, how does that obligate you?

PLAIN *Living*

The distinct roles of boys and girls begin at birth. Announcements in the Amish newspaper, *The Budget*, identify the sex of the baby by its future occupation: "Born to the Jonas Yoders, a little dishwasher named Clara." "The Milo Stotzfuses are the parents of a little woodchopper named Elam." Also, every baby born, even a stillbirth, receives an acknowledgment of a birth announcement in the newspaper.

The Given Word

Swallowing words before you say them is so much better than having to eat them afterward.

Amish Proverb

Norman Erb, an Old Order Amish bishop, is a bear of a man with a thundering voice, sparkling black eyes, a gray-flecked beard, and rather longish hair for an Amish man. The image of Moses springs to mind: perched on the top of Mount Sinai, staff in one hand, stone tablets in another.

Like Moses, Norman often feels the need to remind his church members to take God's commandments seriously. Norman is particularly sensitive to careless words getting tossed around. "Folks don't take their words seriously enough," Norman explains, leaning back in his chair. "Book of Proverbs says, 'In the multitude of words there wanteth not sin: but he that refraineth his lips is wise.'" Wagging a finger in the air for emphasis, he adds, "Words are serious things!"

Norman likes to use stories to make an impact on church members. One of his favorites, he says, is to hit people with this old yarn:

A deacon had to make a visit to a woman in his district who was known for her gossip. So he handed her a bag of feathers and told her to drop a few on the kitchen door of everyone in our church. So she did. Then she brought back the empty bag and handed it to the deacon. The deacon told her, "Now go and get all the feathers collected again."

"What? How can I possibly do that?" she asked. "The wind has blown those feathers every which way!"

"That's very true," the deacon said. "And the very same thing has happened with your words."

The Amish are careful with their words, believing that "needless words" displease God. Wedding vows reflect the serious lifelong commitment assumed between the Amish bride and groom; divorce is virtually unheard of. Profanity is not allowed. Swearing or taking an oath—even in a court of law—is forbidden because a simple yes or no should be sufficient, and "anything beyond this comes from the evil one" (Matt. 5:37).

A confessed sin may never be held against a person—it is dead and buried, never to be spoken of again. In fact, ministers forbid church members to talk about others' confessions or to spread them as gossip; instead, they admonish church members to *fuhgevva und fuhgessa*. Forgive and forget.

Words carry great weight to the Amish. The most significant words an Amish person will utter are when he or she "bends at the knee" and chooses to become baptized as a church member. That one decision weighs heavily on an Amish youth, and from it springs forth all other decisions. Adult baptism is sacred to the Amish, linked to the sacrifices of their ancestors. It can be a very emotional experience, even for a people who keep their feelings under a tight rein.

If an Amish person chooses to leave the church before becoming baptized as a member, they are not under the ban—known as excommunication. Nor will they be shunned. But if they leave after they have become baptized, the ban will be enforced and the consequences of leaving are harsh. A shunned person may not eat at the same table as church members, even family members. That person won't be invited to weddings or community events. Shunning is meant to give one a taste of life without the community, in order to win the person back to full fellowship.

"Oaths are to be made only to God, binding for life," says Norman. All the brightness leaves him, like a cloud swallowing up the sun. "But some do leave. Some leave under the ban." He releases a deep sigh. "They broke a promise, you see."

REFLECTIONS ON FORGIVENESS

So, which is worse, regretting what you said—or regretting what you didn't say?

On the scale of keeping promises, even small ones, where would you rank yourself?

We live in a culture that forever romanticizes change. Students transfer colleges, most people change residences, divorce and remarriage are acceptable. Is there a line to be drawn for change? Consider that change for its own sake rarely leads to peace.

Norman quoted Proverbs 10:19 (KJV). A modern translation (NIV) says, "When words are many, sin is not absent, but he who holds his tongue is wise." How does that ancient wisdom compare to our conviction that everyone has a right to express himself?

PLAIN *Living*

In the late Middle Ages, when Anabaptism began, it was a radical movement, born of the desire to separate church and state—then entirely conjoined—and to baptize only adults, which was then contrary to civil law. The first substantial Anabaptist manifesto was issued in 1527, at Schleitheim, in Switzerland.[4]

Auntie Anne's Soft Pretzels

*A thing long expected takes the form of the unexpected when it
finally comes.*

Amish Proverb

On a fall morning in 1975, nineteen-month-old Angela
darted past her mother, Anne Beiler, to run across the
yard to her grandparents' house. Anne and her husband,
Jonas, lived in a trailer on her parents' farm.

Minutes after Anne saw Angela's golden curls disappear around
the corner, she heard her father scream. Anne's youngest sister,
Fi, was backing out of the barn in a Bobcat tractor. Fi worked for
the family masonry business, scooping sand into the mixer. Fi had
looked carefully around her before backing up the tractor, but
Angela was too quick. The tractor's wheels rolled over the little
toddler.

Anne and her father rushed Angela to the hospital, hoping she
might be resuscitated, but it was too late. Angela had been killed
instantly. When Anne returned to the house, she found her sister
on a sofa, huddled in a fetal position, clutching a pillow to her face.
"Fi's eyes were frantic, wild and scared," Anne said. "She peeked out

from behind the pillow at me and asked if I hated her. She asked if I could ever forgive her."

Instead of blaming her sister, Anne forgave her. "It was never a question. Not then and not since then. I knew it was an accident. Forgiveness entered my heart immediately."

Angela's death became a defining moment in the Beilers' life. Anne and Jonas had been raised Amish. "Life was simple and secure," Anne said. "We were raised knowing life was good. As a child, that's a wonderful thing. But after Angela's death, I started to realize that life was hard. Somehow, I believed that God was harsh too."

She simply did not have the tools to find healing for her grief. "The way we dealt with things, with our family backgrounds, was simply to get on with things, usually in silence," she said. Bottled up grief resulted in Anne's depression and despair, causing a serious threat to her marriage. "We were going our separate ways."

But Jonas wasn't going to let his marriage slip away. Instead of blaming his wife for her transgressions, he forgave her.

"Jonas got down on his knees and asked God what to do," Anne said. "God told him to love me the way God loved him. That forgiveness transformed me." She paused. "Oh, if only every woman could have a husband who loved her the way God loved the church. God's love gave me hope."

Another piece of healing for Anne came through confession. "I had confessed all of my sins to God, but not to anyone else. James 5:16 tells us to confess our sins, one to another. Confession changed my life. I always encourage others to find a safe person with whom they can share their deepest secrets."

Jonas was a mechanic by trade, but Anne said that his true calling was fixing things. People too. He had such an amazing capacity to help others forgive and press on with their lives that he decided to start a counseling ministry, "tuning the engines of broken lives, making them purr again."

And that's where the story of Auntie Anne's Soft Pretzels begins.

To help support Jonas's counseling ministry, Anne worked at and eventually bought a market stand in Downingtown, Pennsylvania. She sold strombolis, pizza, and soft pretzels. Frustrated with the pretzel dough results, she decided to pull pretzels off the menu. "I had spent six weeks tinkering with the recipe, wasting money from trying to get those pretzels just right. I was ready to give up when Jonas asked if he could give it a try." He tried something different with the dough and put them in the oven. Soon, an amazing smell started to circulate around the stand. "The difference in taste between those pretzels and the ones we had been making was indescribable," Anne said. "I couldn't wait to sell them."

Customers couldn't wait to buy them.

By the end of that day, a new business had been launched. "Once again, Jonas came to the rescue," Anne said. Auntie Anne's Soft Pretzels grew like wildfire. Twenty years later, there are over 940 locations in 15 countries.

Anne grew up believing that if she did everything right—if she was completely in God's Word—*then* God would bless her. It took a long time to correct that faulty foundational belief, but it has made all the difference to her. "I'm finally at peace with that bit of theology. I know now that life is hard. But God is good."

Reflections on Forgiveness

Foundational beliefs shape our thinking—right or wrong. Like Anne, did you ever have that foundational belief—God is good but life is hard—backward?

The Amish don't believe that forgiveness is something that happens one time. It continues to happen. Twice a year, the Old

Order Amish hold an all-day communion service. During communion season, church members are urged to make amends with those whom they have offended and seek reconciliation. They take seriously Paul's warning to the Corinthians (1 Cor. 11:27–32). They want everyone to take communion with a clean heart, to "keep short accounts." What benefits do you see in keeping short accounts?

Most relationships, even healthy ones, experience conflicts. Resolving conflicts, though, takes hard work and humility. Is there someone in your life whom you need to forgive? Or someone from whom you need to seek forgiveness?

For the Amish, forgiveness is not an option but an enduring expectation. How does that change your feelings about forgiving someone who has wronged you?

PLAIN *Living*

Twice a year, during communion services, the Old Order Amish church members get down on their knees and, with their bare hands dipping into a bucket of warm water, wash the feet of another Amish person of the same gender.[5]

Good Night, My Son

We can stop forgiving others when Christ stops forgiving us.

Amish Proverb

On Esther Huyard's wedding day to David Smucker, some-one reminded her that "it takes both sunny and rainy days to make a life complete." It was a truth that returned to Esther many times as the young couple raised their family on a dairy farm in Pennsylvania.

A busy road cut between the Smuckers' house and barn. Esther and David were careful to teach their six children how and when to cross the road. At a yard sale one morning, Esther bought a used scooter as a surprise for her children. That evening, the children played a game of treasure hunt as Esther was in the cow stable, doing the milking. The scooter was the treasure, her oldest son whispered to her before zooming off to hide a note for the hunt.

Just minutes later, she heard screams. Five-year-old David Jr., nicknamed Junior, had been hit by a speeding car as he crossed the road, looking for the treasure.

Time passed in a blur as Esther waited for the ambulance to arrive. As she knelt by Junior's still body, she was filled with a calm she couldn't describe. "I felt a presence around me that controlled me. Rather, it was a feeling of awe, that this is sacred. The presence of God was strongly felt. The best way I can explain that controlled feeling is, when your own strength fails, you draw from an inner strength that is not your own. It is divine help."

The driver of the car, a twenty-two-year-old male, panicked. He ran up and down the road crying and yelling, "Now I'm in trouble. Now I'll go to jail."

From deep inside of Esther came a response that she knew didn't originate within her, but from God. She went over to the young driver, hugged him, and told him that Junior had actually told her he was going to heaven soon. "And now he's there!" she reassured the young man, helping to calm him down. "You were just a tool."

The paramedics arrived, found a pulse in Junior—though he was unconscious and unresponsive—and took him to the hospital. By then the police were on the scene, gathering information and helping with traffic control. The police officer took the driver into his patrol car. Esther quietly approached the police officer, her hands folded on her chest as if she were praying. "Please take care of the boy," she said.

The police officer assumed she meant her son, the child who had been hit. He told her that the doctors would do everything they could, but the rest was up to God.

"I mean the driver," she told him. "We forgive him."

At the hospital, Junior was placed on life support. Tests determined that his brain was dead and his internal injuries were severe. The doctor felt that Junior had died instantly, something that Esther had sensed the moment she saw him after the accident. David and Esther agreed to remove his life support and donate his organs, and they prepared to say a tearful, heart-wrenching goodbye to their precious little boy.

Esther never doubted that Junior was in The Beautiful Land, as she called it. She never doubted that he was happy. But her deep faith didn't discount her grief in missing her boy—her grief was severe. She wrote a book that chronicled the year after Junior's death, a hard journey of struggling and healing, called *Good Night, My Son*.

She took comfort in discovering that Junior's death was not wasted. The police officer who helped her at the accident had been estranged from his own son. That very night, he reached out to reconnect to him. There was an inebriated patient who had mocked Esther and David as they arrived at the hospital. When he learned of Junior's death, he apologized to Esther for his behavior. Even then, Esther wondered if she was already beginning to see someone's life touched through her son's death. Other people who had experienced similar loss found the Smuckers and helped them work through their grief, as Esther and David helped them work through theirs.

Long ago, Esther had read a sentence that stuck in her mind: "Never bury the body of your loved one before accepting resurrection in return."

With that belief, she said, life was bearable.

REFLECTIONS ON FORGIVENESS

Esther said that a certain amount of guilt will always follow the death of a child, but she found it only resulted in disturbing any peace of mind concerning his death. She finally came to the conclusion that she could be as careful as possible but life was still dangerous. "The fact remains," she said, "that we are not in control of all things." Getting to this place is hard work—but the result is peace.

In her book, Esther wrote that during the year after Junior's death, she felt she was losing her trust in God and couldn't even pray. The police officer, who had become a friend, told her, "If you feel you are losing your faith and can't pray, then just read the Word of God. Let that do it for you. Read the Psalms."

Do not carry the burden of your grief alone. Seek out a trusted friend, a church group, or a counselor for support.

Esther said she now realizes how futile it is to try to plan the life span of our children and ourselves. "When God calls us home, it doesn't matter what we are doing. We cannot prevent it unless he wills it so." How does that belief—anchored by trust in a loving God—promote peace of mind?

PLAIN *Living*

Despite their ongoing and very real struggles to forgive, the Amish work hard to keep personal disagreements from severing relationships. Indeed, the ritual greetings before the beginning of each church service keep everyone, even adversaries, in touch. As the women gather in a circle, they greet one another with a kiss. The men, gathering in a separate circle, shake hands. These rituals help to maintain relationships that may otherwise rupture.[6]

Part 5

The Sovereignty of God

You cannot change life—because God on high,
controls this world with an all-seeing eye.
He makes the calls and you're never alone;
all's well in heaven and God's on the throne.

Amish Proverb

Election Night 2008

It is Tuesday, November 4, 2008, the day our country is going to elect a new president. Throughout the day, I check in with news sources to listen to exit polls and election results. A little before 5 p.m., I pick up the leash to take the dog for a walk before the first polls close on the East Coast. After all, this is an important day for our country. Whoever wins the election, there will be a "first" in office. Either our country's first African American president or our country's first female vice president. An historic night.

Earlier in the day I had left a message on an answering machine for Samuel, an Old Order Amish bishop, a man who has been kind to answer some questions for me about Amish ways. Just as my hand reaches for the doorknob, the phone rings. My phone's caller ID pops up with Samuel's name, so I put down the dog leash (sorry, pup) and grab my notebook and pen, eager to connect with him. It's always fun to talk with Samuel. I learn so much from him. Not thirty seconds later, Samuel makes a remark that seems so right, so grounded, so piercing in its simple wisdom, that I feel a catch in my heart.

Samuel: "Hello, Suzanne. I was going stargazing tonight and stopped by the phone shanty to pick up my messages. Thought I'd return your call."

Suzanne: "Samuel, do you mean to tell me that the entire country is glued to the television tonight and you're going stargazing?"

Samuel: "Well, you see, Venus and Jupiter are moving close together this month. . . ." (He then went on to describe the alignment of the planets with great enthusiasm and detail. I could barely keep up! Remember, this is a man with an eighth-grade education. But that doesn't mean his education stopped at eighth grade.)

I stop taking notes, a little stunned. Think about it. Most Americans (myself included) were thoroughly immersed in the moment, on a temporal event (albeit an important one) that would come and go.

What a *profound* comparison of our two cultures! We are both Americans. We are both Christians. We had both voted that day (he even told me for whom he voted). He knows all about the election and its consequences. I ask him where he gets his news and he says, "My daughter subscribes to *Newsweek* and gives me her old issues, and I read a local daily newspaper, but it's pretty feeble." He has strong reasons for the candidate whom he supports, and he lists out his reasoning, apologizing if it conflicts with my party affiliation.

No doubt about it, Samuel cares about this election. He voted. But then he went stargazing.

Samuel's eyes are fixed on the heavens.

On the eternal view.

On a sovereign God.

Stargazing isn't a one-time "antidote to election anxiety" for Samuel. Actually, I don't think he feels any anxiety about the election at all. Stargazing is a way of life for him, a metaphor. So are long walks in the woods. He keeps a pair of binoculars with him for bird-watching as he plows the fields in spring. "Skywatching has its rewards," he says. He has never once gone on a walk in which he didn't see or find something exciting or interesting.

Samuel sees God in every aspect of creation, large and small, from the recycling efforts of the dung beetle to the red-tailed hawk that soars above his fields on thermals of warm air, searching for a down-on-his-luck cottontail. "The God who created all of this beauty and grace must be a wonderful and loving Being," he says, meaning it with his whole heart.

And such a God, Samuel believes, is able to bring all things together to his glory.

As I hang up the phone with Samuel, I pick up the dog's leash (oh happy dog!) and take her for a long, long walk. I hear the hoot of a great horned owl, trying to woo a mate. I watch the late afternoon sky change from bruised blue to velvety black, dotted with diamonds. The day's concerns, even a day with a national election, seem so small and unimportant under this sky. Worries lift, floating up off my shoulders and disappearing into the night. I decide that I will not watch the election results, after all. I can wait and read about our next president in tomorrow's paper. And I promise myself to make a daily appointment with nature to remind myself of Whose capable hands are in charge of this earth.

What a difference it makes when we lift our eyes upward and fix them on God's heavens.

"Those who are wise will shine like the brightness of the heavens, and those who lead many to righteousness, like the stars for ever and ever" (Dan. 12:3).

No Sunday Sales

God puts the church in the world. Satan seeks to put the world in the church.

Amish Proverb

Te small handwritten sign at the end of a long gravel drive-way states: "Eggs & Quilts." Below it is added: "No Sunday Sales." That signage is a broad indicator that you have stumbled onto an Amish-owned farm or shop.

On this Saturday afternoon, the Graber family—who lives at the end of that driveway—is working steadily to prepare for Sunday church, the backbone of the Amish life. The two oldest boys scrub down the buggies, brush them out, and clean off the windshields. Debbie Graber, the oldest girl in the family, has taken down the laundry from the clothesline, ironed, folded, and put it all away. Debbie's mother has prepared a light meal for Sunday supper. The house has been cleaned. The week's work is done.

For the Amish, most of Saturday afternoon is geared to preparing for a Sabbath's rest. They safeguard Sunday to make it a day free of all but necessary work, like milking dairy cows and caring for animals. Even if the oats are ready to be harvested, the chore will wait. Even if the hay is cut and rain is coming, it will remain on the field until Monday morning. Sunday is sacred.

For over three hundred years, the Amish have devoted Sunday to worship and family. By observing the Sabbath, they believe that they honor God. They don't take their freedom to worship for granted. Such freedom came at a steep price.

In the 1500s and 1600s, the Anabaptists faced severe persecution by the religious and governmental authorities. They were arrested if found to be conducting religious activities outside the established Protestant and Catholic churches, so they worshiped in hideaways—not unlike the first few centuries of Christianity when believers gathered in catacombs. If discovered, Anabaptists were tortured and executed. The book *Martyr's Mirror*, found in every Amish home, describes the hardships endured by their ancestors.

Today, the Amish hold their twice-a-month church service in homes. The church, they feel, is a body of believers, not a single place. Every church family takes a turn hosting church, usually once a year. When it's a family's turn to host church, the wife's mother, sisters, sisters-in-law, and neighbors may spend two or three days helping to clean the house from top to bottom.

A benchwagon—holding just about everything but the preacher—transports hymnals and benches for seating at the service. Homes are built or adjusted with large doors to open the interior to accommodate a large gathering for such a service. The Amish have the conviction that smaller is better; when the church grows too large to meet in a home, they split the district into two and add new ministers and a deacon.

The Amish worship service lasts three or more hours. Females sit on one side, males on the other. When babies cry, church members tolerate it; ministers simply preach over the crying. From the very start, children are trained to remain quiet during the service, though a plate of cookies or pretzels will be handed down the line. Sharing a simple meal together—prepared in advance and light enough to require little cleanup—follows every church service. The afternoon is reserved for visits with neighbors and friends.

Sunday afternoons and evenings in the Amish community are traditionally the social times for the "young folk"—those over the age of sixteen. Whoever hosted church that morning will invite the young folk to come back to their home on Sunday evening to share a light supper, play some volleyball—often, two buggies lined up with a clothesline strung between them serve as net and posts—and later, they will sing for a couple of hours. Sometimes, as many as fifty to one hundred Amish teens will gather, drawing from other back-and-forth church districts, clogging town streets with open courting buggies.

A manageable crowd, for the Amish.

These gatherings become a way for Amish teens to meet potential romantic interests. Debbie's older brother, Jake, met his bride, Rose, at his cousin's singing. For three years, Jake traveled over ten miles by buggy to see Rose, often not returning home until morning milking time.

The Amish cherish and safeguard their Sundays. "It's my favorite day of the week," said Debbie. "Even the off-Sundays. I like spending the day with the family or friends, or just reading my books."

Sunday, for the Amish, is a day set apart. It's a day of renewal: for the soul and for the community.

REFLECTIONS ON THE SOVEREIGNTY OF GOD

Church is such an important ritual to the Amish that they arrange their life around it. What place does church hold in your life? What specific responsibilities do you have in your faith community?

We all need time to let our souls catch up. Take inventory of your Sundays over the past few weeks. What's your routine?

Do you feel more rested, more at peace, more attuned to God as a result of the way you spend your Sundays? Or is it just another day?

Sunday, it seems, has turned into a business-as-usual day. Church gets squeezed in between our kids' sporting events and grocery shopping for the upcoming week. It's not easy to set Sunday apart, with a focus on worship, rest, and recreation. In a way, honoring the Sabbath in our modern times takes more trust than it used to, when the rest of the world took a day off too. Trust is required to believe that God will provide the time, as needed, to complete responsibilities. "Keep the Sabbath day holy. Don't pursue your own interests on that day. . . . Then the LORD will be your delight," God says in the book of Isaiah (28:13–14 NLT).

Sunday might not work for you or your family. Is there another day that could be safeguarded as a Sabbath rest?

PLAIN *Living*

The most conservative of the major affiliations is the Swartzentruber Amish. The Swartzentruber Amish split from the Old Order Amish in about 1913 over how strictly shunning (*Meidung*) should be carried out. The Swartzentruber Amish are known today because they are also the most traditional in their refusal to use most forms of modern technology in the home and on the farm.[1]

Only God Fires Ministers

Never doubt in the dark what God has shown you in the light.

Amish Proverb

In one day, William Zook lost three family members in a house fire. William's mother and sister lived in the top floor of his brother's farmhouse. The two women had a hot plate, Coleman camp stove style, in their room—a convenience that suited them nicely. They didn't have to go down to the kitchen whenever a cup of tea sounded good, which was often.

One night, something too close to the hot plate started to smolder and burn, unnoticed. The fire reached a gas line in the attic and exploded, killing William's mother and sister. "My brother went up to open the door to help them," William said, "but he was instantly killed when the door opened."

William wasn't complaining or feeling sorry for himself; he was just telling his story. A very sad story. "A man should not grieve overmuch," he quoted, "for that is a complaint against God."

Dressed in Sunday black broadfalls, vest, and coat, William had eyes as dark as coal. His wiry beard ringed his round chin. He was confined to a wheelchair after a knee operation resulted in a serious staph infection. "That made my hips go bad," he explained. "So now

193

I'm stuck in this old chair." He patted the arms of the wheelchair. "But I still preach, whenever it's my turn," he added.

Now in his sixties, William has been a minister for the better part of thirty years. "I was only twenty-nine when I drew the lot." He laughed. "I won the lottery!" Although it does happen, it's rare that such a young man would become a minister.

A typical Amish church district has a bishop, two ministers, and a deacon. Those leaders are chosen through a divine lottery. The only way to become a minister is to be "hit" by the "casting of the lot," just the way Judas Iscariot's replacement was made in the book of Acts. Nominations for the position are whispered to the existing minister from the members, including women, though only married men can be nominated. It's a system to ensure that a person of good reputation will become a religious leader. "The Ordnung [rules for living] expect each man to know the Bible well so that he'll be prepared if the lot falls on him," explained William.

Three to five people nominated William, he recalled, then a slip of paper with "You are the one" on it was put in an *Ausbund*—the Amish hymnal. As many hymnals as there were nominees were placed on a bench in front of the congregation. Only one hymnal held the slip of paper. With a divine nod, the man who picked the lot became the selected minister.

William remembered being overcome with a great sadness, a common response to this overwhelming responsibility. "I felt the weight of it when I drew the lot," William said. "I knew I would be the one getting the slip. I had already felt the call, years earlier. I had a sense it would be coming one day."

Unlike a Protestant pastor or Catholic priest, Amish ministers serve without pay and without formal training. William has had to squeeze in the obligations of being a minister while still managing his farm and caring for his large family. Sunday sermons are long, biblically explicit, detailed . . . and without notes. Ministers must spend long hours in preparation for their Sunday delivery. Habitually, William spends time on Saturday afternoon to prepare for the Sunday meetings through prayer, study, and Scripture reading. While they are viewed with great respect from the church members, ministers are expected to lead a life worthy of the calling. That includes their children, an added pressure on families. "All of my children have been baptized in the Amish church," William said, pleased. "But it's not easy being the children of a minister. Never has been, never will."

When an Amish man draws the lot, it is a lifetime appointment. With a grin, William added, "Only the Lord God can fire a minister."

REFLECTIONS ON THE SOVEREIGNTY OF GOD

William says that every Amish man is expected to know the Bible well so that he will be prepared if the lot falls on him. How well prepared are you for a task God might ask of you?

William suffered an unimaginable loss but never seemed to doubt the sovereignty and goodness of God. It doesn't mean he was insulated from feeling grief, but his peace was deep and stabilizing. What foundational truth was William's peace based on?

Helen Keller is quoted as saying, "I do not want the peace which passeth understanding. I want the understanding which bringeth peace." How would you describe the difference?

Peace is not simply the absence of difficulties. God's peace can exist even in the middle of problems. Where can we find this peace? (Look up Phil. 4:6–7.)

PLAIN *Living*

O Gott Vater, wir loben Dich (O Father God, we praise thee) is a hymn that is also used at the ordination services of a deacon, minister, or bishop. At this hymn page, a special paper will be found in the Ausbund songbook of God's chosen servant. The second verse of this hymn will be read to this chosen servant before he is officially ordained.

Second verse:

Open the mouth of Thy servants, Lord,
And give them wisdom also,
That they may rightly speak Thy Word
Which encourages a devout life
And serves to glorify Thee;
Give us a desire for such nourishment.
This is our petition.[2]

The Cycle of Life

We are not promised skies always blue, but a Helper to see us through.

Amish Proverb

O n an unusually warm spring evening, Noah King was in the barn, wiping and cleaning his tools, when he heard Annie, his wife, call out that dinner was ready. Through the large barn door, Noah could spot his six children emerging out of different corners of the yard, interrupted in their game of hide-and-seek.

There should have been eight, come May, he thought sadly. *But who am I to question the ways of the Lord?*

Just a few months before, Annie had been pregnant with identical twin girls. In winter, the doctor discovered that one of the babies wasn't receiving enough nutrients to grow. Annie was taken to a reputed children's hospital for a specialized procedure to correct the imbalance. The procedure was successful, and Annie was able to return home.

After Christmas, on a cold December day, Annie's water broke. English friends drove Annie and Noah to the hospital. Annie had a Caesarean section and both baby girls were delivered alive but hopelessly premature.

That evening, the smaller baby died. Her body was taken out of the intensive care unit, where her sister lay fighting for her life, and brought in to be held by her mother for a last goodbye. Family members had gathered to give support to Annie and Noah, including all six of their children. Everyone had a chance to say goodbye to the little girl, gently caressing the tiny ivory body, not much larger than the palm of a man's hand. The baby's eyelids were transparently thin with fine lines of blue veins still showing. The little rosebud mouth was slightly open. Even her two-year-old sister held her and whispered loving words to her.

A few hours later, a doctor arrived to tell them that the other baby had died. Again, the entire family held the still, little body. The hospital, experienced with Amish ways, provided white clothing and white caps for the babies. A service in the private chapel was held for the girls, and the burial occurred by late afternoon, close to dusk. Noah wanted it that way. He wanted his entire family to be together, to experience the cycle of life. *We will heal more easily if we share the loss,* he thought. And knew it to be true. Together, the family grieved. Together, they were healing.

But as the month of May came, and with it the babies' actual due date, Noah felt a wave of fresh grief. He knew Annie felt it too. He had seen the dried tears on her cheeks in the morning.

Noah finished wiping off the last of his tools, brushed the oil off of his hands, and went in to join his family for the evening meal.

Grief was just plain hard, he decided, but the Lord's ways were always best.

Reflections on the Sovereignty of God

Does it seem as if our culture has lost an understanding of the "cycle of life"? What benefits might there be in not overprotecting our children from the reality of death?

What circumstances are you struggling to accept? Consider the need to formally "bury" that loss, allowing yourself the chance to grieve.

One Amish family bore the loss of two sons—an infant through Sudden Infant Death Syndrome (SIDS) and a five-year-old through a car accident. The father reminded his family that, as much as they wished the boys were still with them, they will not come back. "The important thing we want to keep in mind," he told them, "is this: we want to go to them." How does that father's statement change one's focus from grief to hope? Why should we learn what Scripture has to tell us about heaven? How real is heaven to you?

PLAIN *Living*

A new Amish settlement is established somewhere in the United States or in Ontario, Canada, every five weeks on average.[3]

The Good Samaritan

You can tell how big a person is by what it takes to discourage him.

Amish Proverb

Rachel faced the ceiling in a bed in the emergency room of the local hospital, plucking at the loose strings of her prayer cap, hoping the doctor would give her good news. She smoothed some loose strands of gray hair and tucked them in her prayer cap. She winced as she brushed her face with her hand. The knot of a bruise was developing on her cheek.

Her mind drifted back to the accident. Earlier this morning, Rachel had been hanging laundry on the clothesline in her yard when she saw a runaway horse galloping toward her farm. Dropping the clothespin that she held between her lips, she called out for Eli, her husband, to come out from the barn to help. Thinking fast, Rachel knew that if she could get the horse cornered in their yard, she could catch him. It wouldn't be the first time she had caught a runaway horse. Her father bred horses; she was raised with them.

But she should have paid closer attention to the woodchuck holes in the grass. Here she was, a woman on the shady side of fifty-nine, running like a schoolgirl after a loose buggy horse.

And it wasn't even her horse!

When the doctor asked her how the injury happened, he smiled and called her a regular Good Samaritan. That was right before he held up the X-ray against the screen and showed her where she had fractured her leg in two separate places. He then informed her that she would need surgery to put screws into the bones to hold them in place. After that, he said, the leg would be set in a cast.

Rachel frowned. She didn't like the idea of having a limb stuck in a cast. Too long a time to be immobilized. Even worse, the doctor told her she would need to be in a wheelchair. When she heard that news, she let out a deep sigh as her shoulders slumped.

"Well, there's a bright spot, Mom," Eli said, casting a sideways glance at his wife. "I'll be taller than you for a little while." A slight, small man with wire-rimmed glasses, his tall, sturdy wife usually towered over him. It was a topic about which he had received a generous dose of good-natured teasing over the years.

The doctor smiled as he yanked the X-ray off the screen. Rachel was not as easily amused. She planted a fist on her hip, a sure sign she was not in the mood for Eli's jokes. "I don't have time to be stuck in a wheelchair," she said in a tone of someone who was running late for an appointment with the president of the United States.

Suddenly, her grim mood lifted. "You know, Dad," she told Eli, "I think I can still work from the wheelchair. The kitchen is big enough that I can scoot it around, especially if we push the table against the wall."

The doctor laughed out loud. "Now, Rachel, why not think of this as a little break from the daily grind? Kind of an enforced vacation. It wasn't your fault. It's just one of those things."

"Life just has to be lived as it comes," Rachel answered, lifting her chin a notch. "Bad things happen, like broken legs. And good things, like weddings to plan and babies being born. It's not up to us to question God's ways. But life still has to go on."

"Rachel, you're going to have to take it easy for a while," the doctor warned her. He looked to Eli for support.

"You did plenty of work today, Mom," Eli pointed out, chuckling. He turned to the doctor. "She caught the horse."

REFLECTIONS ON THE SOVEREIGNTY OF GOD

The Amish don't expect life to be trouble free. They believe the biblical explanation that "the rain falls on the just and the unjust." When faced with difficulties, they quickly move on, adjusting to the circumstances. Even from a wheelchair, Rachel was plotting how to continue to work and contribute to her household. Are the circumstances in your life difficult? How can you respond with positive measures?

When the good you do doesn't seem appreciated or even noticed, how do you feel? For whom are you doing it?

Don't fritter away precious moments by dwelling on hardships—moments that become spoiled, spent, or sullied. Instead give thanks in all things, as that is the will of God. Go back over the last few days and think of the things that have happened in your life, thanking God for them.

PLAIN *Living*

Traditionally, the Amish do not accept old-age assistance or public assistance of any kind. Neither do they buy life insurance. Needy older persons are aided by relatives. Should a close relative be incompetent or unwilling, the church will come to the assistance of the elderly.[4]

Amische Lieder (Amish Music)

The higher a man gets in divine grace, the lower he will be in his own esteem.

Amish Proverb

After a simple breakfast of cereal, toast with homemade raspberry jam, and freshly squeezed orange juice, eighty-year-old Mose Yoder rose to his feet. Turning as slowly as a weathervane on a breezeless day, he opened a cabinet drawer behind him and pulled out a harmonica. He lifted the harmonica to his pale lips, a signal to his wife, Eva. She put down her dish towel and joined him for the benediction to the meal. Wheezing a little as he blew through the pipes, he began, and a slow and recognizable melody soon emerged: "Amazing Grace." After playing a verse, Mose put down the harmonica. He and Eva sang a verse in German, then again in English. Smiling and unembarrassed, their reedy voices joined together in harmony, a harmony that came from living together for nearly sixty years.

Harmony is only used among the Amish for "out of church" singing. Mose's harmonica remains at home, tucked away in his cabinet drawer. Music sung at church is entirely a cappella. Instruments are not used in worship, for that would be considered ostentatious and contrary to the spirit of humility. "I love harmony," Mose said. "But in church, we all sing in one voice, in unison, so no one stands out. One person shouldn't stand out beyond another."

Singing is a deeply rooted, vital part of the worship experience for the Amish, secondary only to the preaching of the Word. It evokes the deepest emotions of the human spirit. Every worship service begins and ends with a hymn.

The congregation sings from the *Ausbund*—a term meaning "selection" or "anthology"—a hymnal with only printed words. Tunes, learned by memory and passed down through the centuries, are sung not with many voices but with one. The Amish alone have kept the ancient musical tradition. For three hundred years they have sung these hymns in just this way, and so it will always be.

The slow tunes, or *langsam Weis*, as the Amish call them, were composed in prison. The verses were meant to be sung and committed to memory. It's likely that the prisoners shouted them to each other in secluded dungeons. The slow and doleful singing prompted historian Joseph Yoder to suggest that the tunes were derived from the Gregorian chant. Some of the hymns can take as long as twenty minutes to sing. Although the Amish sing only four or five verses, some hymns have as many as thirty-seven verses. Each word is stretched out into a chanting cadence. Sung slow and unchanging, always together. One flesh, one mind, one spirit.

In singing these hymns, an Amish person is reminded of their heritage of faith. And their hope.

Mose and Eva sing their hymn as a morning and evening ritual, a pattern to start and end each day. Mose may not have many more days. His lips are blue, his skin color is gray. He has already had one heart attack and two serious operations. He finally decided to toss out the medications—which were only making him sicker, he realized—and trust his remaining time on earth to the Lord. "I've already lived two years past the doctor's prediction," he said, looking a little pleased. "But I get winded easily now. I'm just happy to be alive.

"I'm ready to go," he added. "But only the Lord knows the day." Mose shrugged. "Whatever," he added, sounding a lot like an English teen. He smiled slightly, at peace with his future.

Mose and Eva lift their faces slightly, eyes closed in reverence as they sing. Their tinny voices aren't exactly easy on the ears. But they just keep singing, unconcerned by the fact that their voices are neither beautiful nor professional.

After all, they're not singing for themselves.

REFLECTIONS ON THE SOVEREIGNTY OF GOD

What kind of traditions does your family have? How can you use them to experience true peace?

Singing can evoke the deepest emotions of the human spirit. Find ways to bring uplifting music into your life today.

Some of the classic hymns of our faith describe great doctrinal truths or tell the gospel story. Memorizing hymns can be a painless way of calling God's Word to mind, as the Bible encourages us to do. Have you thought of ways to encourage your family to memorize hymns? Here's one suggestion: the next time you take a long car ride, consider trying to commit to memory *Amazing Grace* or *Great Is Thy Faithfulness*.

PLAIN *Living*

"O Gott Vater, wir loben Dich" ("O Father God, We Praise Thee") is the second song sung at every Amish worship service. It is also used at many Amish gatherings as a song of comfort, hope, and guidance, sung with a faster tune. It is a prayer of praise and a plea for spiritual desire, nourishment, and admonition through the service.[5]

Be Ye Separate

Opportunity may knock once, but temptation bangs on your front door forever.

Amish Proverb

Growing up in the late 1930s in Kalona, Iowa, Fred Miller remembered that his Old Order Amish family interacted often with English neighbors. "I was raised in the country," he said. "We growed up poor, like everybody else. We had enough to eat, and just a few pieces of clothes. I went to a public high school and had lots of friends who were English." The neighboring farm to Fred's family was a large English family with kids who were playmates to Fred and his siblings. "All of the neighbors helped each other out. We was all in the same boat. We all harvested crops together."

Until, Fred said, the television entered the American home.

In the early '50s, Fred's English neighbors bought one of the first televisions. "We went over and watched it some," Fred said. "It was at that grainy, black-and-white stage, when the tube took a while to warm up. Hard on the eyes. My mom and dad decided that was enough of that. They didn't let us near a television. They could see it was a misleading thing. We wasn't allowed to go over to that family's house no more, even though they was Lutheran. That television really drove us apart."

Looking back, Fred is convinced his mother made the right decision. "I think it's a good idea to be separate. It's important to abstain from worldly things. Keeps us from getting contaminated."

Two years ago, Fred suffered a stroke that left him paralyzed on his right side. With physical therapy twice a week, he has regained strength and mobility. "There's a television on while I'm at the therapist. Hooboy, the kinds of things that are on that screen today! We got so many more temptations now than we did in the fifties. And the Internet is a whole lot worse. My folks could see that nothing good would come of it, and they was right. I couldn't have a TV in my house and believe in God." Fred said that his mother always told him, "Whatever you fill your mind with, fills your heart. And whatever fills your heart, it comes out of your mouth."

Fred explained that the Amish conviction to be unhooked from the ways of the modern world dates back to the time of Moses, leading the Israelites out of Egypt and into the Promised Land—separate and isolated. "Our forefathers set it up that way, from the Old Country."

The Amish believe that the secular world is filled with temptation, and it is important to avoid those temptations by remaining as separate as possible. They cite a verse from 2 Corinthians that admonishes, "Be ye not unequally yoked together with unbelievers" and ends with the command, "Come out from among them and be ye separate" (2 Cor. 6:14, 17 KJV). It is the framework on which they've built their lives. "It's one of the reasons we keep using Deitsch," Fred said. "It's our own language from the old world."

While the Israelites had the luxury of a wide-open desert to find isolation, the Amish live squeezed in among the English, not in cloistered colonies. Amazingly, the Amish are part *of* a fast-paced, modern society but somehow manage to not be completely *in* it. They deliberately restrict their dependence on the modern world.

They live off the grid of public utilities and create their own energy with solar panels, batteries, propane gas, windmills, and watermills. Although they do use English doctors and hospitals, they do not have medical or life insurance because it would require joining with others who are not Amish. Instead, the church pools money to help families cover medical costs of their members. The Amish do not participate in Social Security or accept any government money, perceiving it as a "handout" (they do pay local, state, and federal taxes).

More important than restrictions are what the Amish have chosen to emphasize: their deeply cherished faith and the well-being of their community. Faith is the living stream from which all things spring forth.

"We use that or we lose that," Fred said, stroking the thick white beard that spilled down his chest like a waterfall. "If we lose that, it's trouble."

REFLECTIONS ON THE SOVEREIGNTY OF GOD

Ask yourself—are the reasons you watch TV and surf the Web helping you as you think they will? What would happen if you turned them off?

The use of Pennsylvania Dutch (Deitsch) as their first language (English and German are their second and third languages) helps the Amish maintain their distinct identity and is a constant reminder of their European Anabaptist heritage. What reminders do you have to be set apart?

How seriously do you take temptations? Do you think there's a danger of growing desensitized to some temptations?

What might be some choices you could make that would allow for greater peace in your life?

PLAIN *Living*

Over fifty years ago, sociologists predicted that the Amish would soon be absorbed into the larger society. The Amish population has [more than] tripled since 1950 and the assimilation rate has not changed significantly.[6]

Epilogue

Sticky Fingers

Before we can pray "Thy Kingdom come," we must pray "My kingdom go."

Amish Proverb

It is a blistering hot June evening and I am stuck in a traffic jam, retrieving my dad from his latest escapade after receiving a call from the police with his whereabouts. My dad is in the mid-stages of Alzheimer's disease. He has a knack of finding ways to sneak out of his board and care facility, hitchhike with strangers, and end up in unusual places. Today, it is a Wal-Mart, thirty minutes away.

I feel enormously relieved that Dad is safe. These escapes have been frightening. For me, not for Dad. He is unconcerned about the panic he creates. He has already forgotten it. He doesn't know my name, but he does like to point out which road I should take and when to turn, often encouraging me to sail through red lights. Dad's directions are dangerous. He's always wrong but never in doubt.

As my car crawls along the freeway, resentment starts bubbling over. My day has already been overloaded. My college kids had just arrived home for the summer, and I was hoping to prepare a special family dinner. I hadn't been able to snag any time to write that day; my mind was still preoccupied with a looming deadline. And now the day is wrapping up with Dad's breakout.

The consuming requirements of my dad's illness have been creating a growing frustration. Obligations to him always seem to come at the worst moment, forcing me to push aside my own family's needs. My dad, who was always a delightful person, has become an enormous inconvenience. And as his disease marches forward, it's only going to get worse.

My mind drifts to the Amish. When I visited Amish communities, I asked many how they handled a relative with Alzheimer's. Without exception, they replied that they took care of their elderly at home. Granted, they have enormous families who live locally and share the caregiving role. Even with support, Alzheimer's is no cakewalk. One Amish woman cared for her mother for seven years. Another was up in the night, changing bedsheets for her mother, every forty-five minutes for over a year. But I never detected a hint of self-pity as these women shared their stories with me. "It's just what we do," they said, as if that explained everything—their patience, their kindness, their dedication.

These women believe that all of life's circumstances are given by God, good ones as well as hard ones. Even Alzheimer's. They yield to things out of their control. They don't struggle and fight against them, like I do.

So as my car idles in that traffic jam, I wonder how those two Amish women might handle this exasperating situation. I know, I know; they wouldn't be in a car, they would be in a buggy. I mean the yielding part, the interior repose that works to align itself with the mind of Christ.

I can imagine them saying that it is my time to give back to my father for all he has done for me. That there are things I will be learning in this experience, marathon that it is. They would point out that it is an opportunity for me to develop and express a selfless love. And they would remind me that my father, even in his condition, matters to God. His soul is intact even as his mind is fading.

An entirely unexpected thing happens as I ponder the imaginary conversation of my Amish ladies, spouting their wisdom to me. Sweet memories pop into my mind of Dad in his better days . . . dropping by my house on a hot summer day with popsicles for my children, helping us paint after we remodeled the house. Or when he encouraged me, as a teen, to attend a private college although the tuition bill would create personal hardship for him.

As these memories displace my frustration, I feel the traffic-jam stress dissipate. In its place is a tender patience for Dad, just as he is. I actually feel calmer, more relaxed, more open to God's way of thinking, though my circumstances have not changed one iota. The traffic is just as bad and the sun is even worse—it has intensified its glare directly onto my windshield like a magnifying glass. When I stop struggling against my circumstances, I actually *feel* benefits. What might seem on the surface a hopeless surrender, white flag raised, becomes transformed into the powerful mystery of yielding.

If there is one thing I have learned through the writing of this book, it is that taking my sticky fingers off of the controls and yielding to God is a good thing, a *wonderful* thing. It's not passive, it's hard work! And it takes practice. But through the example of my Amish friends—whose lives are embroidered with daily reminders of their dependence on God—I am learning to trust God in a more meaningful way.

And on the heels of yielding comes the peace of Christ.

Notes

Introduction

1. Uncle Amos, "Become Amish?" *Small Farmer's Journal* 17, no. 3 (1993).

Simplicity

1. Donald B. Kraybill, *The Amish of Lancaster County* (Mechanicsburg, PA: Stackpole Books, 2008), 50.

2. Gene Logsdon, "What Does Progress Mean?" *The Draft Horse Journal*, Autumn 2003.

3. Jon Kinney, ed., *The Amish of Holmes County: A Culture, a Religion, a Way of Life* (Orrville, OH: Spectrum Publications, 1996), 62.

4. Rebecca Mabry, *The Amish of Illinois' Heartland* (Champlain, IL: News-Gazette, 2008), 46.

5. Tom Schachtman, *Rumspringa: To Be or Not to Be Amish* (New York: North Point Press, 2006), 176.

6. Erik Wesner, *Amish America*, www.amishamerica.typepad.com, June 21, 2007.

7. David R. Bassett Jr., Patrick L. Schneider, and Gertrude E. Huntington, "Physical Activity in an Old Order Amish Community," *Medicine & Science in Sports & Exercise*, vol. 36, no. 1 (2004): 79–85.

8. Evadnie Rampersaud, et al., "Physical Activity and the Association of Common *FTO* Gene Variants with Body Mass Index and Obesity," *Archives of Internal Medicine*, vol. 168, no. 16 (2008): 1791–97.

9. John Hostetler, *Amish Society* (Baltimore, MD: The Johns Hopkins University Press, 1993), 163.

10. www.lehmans.com.

Time

1. Sue Bender, *Plain and Simple: A Woman's Journey to the Amish* (New York: HarperCollins, 1991), 130.
2. Brad Igou, comp., *The Amish in Their Own Words* (Scottdale, PA: Herald Press, 1999), 358.
3. Joe Wittmer, PhD, *The Gentle People: An Inside View of Amish Life* (Washington, IN: Black Buggy, 2007), 80.
4. Jon Kinney, ed., *The Amish of Holmes County: A Culture, a Religion, a Way of Life* (Orrville, OH: Spectrum Publications, 1996), 60.
5. Schachtman, *Rumspringa*, 177.
6. Hostetler, *Amish Society*, 242.
7. Ibid.
8. Schachtman, *Rumspringa*, 14.
9. Hostetler, *Amish Society*, 168.
10. Mabry, *Amish of Illinois' Heartland*, 63.

Community

1. Kraybill, *Amish of Lancaster County*, 25.
2. Author interview with Dr. Donald B. Kraybill, April 18, 2008.
3. Wittmer, *Gentle People*, 127.
4. Mabry, *Amish of Illinois' Heartland*, 85.
5. Hostetler, *Amish Society*, 160.
6. Ibid., 136.
7. Ibid., 188.
8. Ibid., 189.
9. Esther Smucker, *Good Night, My Son* (Morgantown, PA: Masthof Press, 1995), 70.
10. Kinney, *Amish of Holmes County*, 59.
11. Mabry, *Amish of Illinois' Heartland* , 55.
12. Schachtman, *Rumspringa*, 48.
13. Ibid., 226.
14. Mabry, *Amish of Illinois' Heartland*, 63.
15. Kinney, *Amish of Holmes County*, 42.

Forgiveness

1. Schachtman, *Rumspringa*, 47.
2. Fred Luskin, *Forgive for Good* (San Francisco: HarperOne, 2003).
3. Schachtman, *Rumspringa*, 125.
4. Ibid., 27.
5. Wittmer, *Gentle People*, 22.
6. Donald B. Kraybill, Steven M. Nolt, and David L. Weaver-Zercher, *Amish Grace: How Forgiveness Transcended Tragedy* (San Francisco: John Wiley & Sons, 2007), 121.

The Sovereignty of God

1. George M. Kreps, Joseph F. Donnermeyer, and Marty W. Kreps, *A Quiet Moment in Time: A Contemporary View of Amish Society* (Sugarcreek, OH: Carlisle Press, 1997), 43.

2. *"Es Pennsilfaanisch Deitsch Eck,"* *The Budget*, May 7, 2008.

3. Schachtman, *Rumspringa*, 25.

4. Hostetler, *Amish Society*, 168.

5. *"Es Pennsilfaanisch Deitsch Eck,"* *The Budget*, May 7, 2008.

6. Hostetler, *Amish Society*, viii.

Recommended Reading

There are many excellent books about the Amish that provide the reader with accurate information and give a greater understanding of the Amish and their culture. Those listed here have been reviewed by the author and represent a personal recommendation.

The Diary
PO Box 98
Gordonville, PA 17529
Published monthly

Pathway Publishers
258ON—250W
LaGrange, IN 46761
(publishes *Family Life, Young Companion, Bulletin Board*)

The Budget
PO Box 249
Sugarcreek, OH 44681
Published weekly

Amish Grace: How Forgiveness Transcended Tragedy by Donald B. Kraybill, Steven M. Nolt, David L. Weaver-Zercher (John Wiley & Sons, 2007).

Amish Society by John Hostetler (The Johns Hopkins University Press, 1993).

Great Possessions: An Amish Farmer's Journal by David Kline (North Point Press, 1990).

Lessons for Living: A Practical Approach to Daily Life from the Amish Community by Joseph F. Donnermeyer, George M. Kreps, and Marty W. Kreps (Carlisle Press, 1999).

A Quiet Moment in Time: A Contemporary View of Amish Society by George M. Kreps, Joseph F. Donnermeyer, and Marty W. Kreps (Carlisle Press, 1997).

Rumspringa: To Be or Not to Be Amish by Tom Schachtman (North Point Press, 2006).

Scratching the Woodchuck: Nature on an Amish Farm by David Kline (University of Georgia Press, 1999).

The Amish in Their Own Words compiled by Brad Igou (Herald Press, 1999).

The Amish of Lancaster County by Donald B. Kraybill (Stackpole Books, 2008).

The Gentle People: An Inside View of Amish Life by Joe Wittmer, PhD (Black Buggy, 2007).

The Riddle of Amish Culture by Donald B. Kraybill (The Johns Hopkins University Press, 1989).

Recommended Documentary

The Amish: How They Survive by Burton Buller (Black Hat Distributors, Ltd., 2005).

Suzanne Woods Fisher's interest in the Anabaptist cultures can be directly traced to her grandfather, W. D. Benedict, who was raised in the Old Order German Baptist Brethren Church in Franklin County, Pennsylvania. Benedict left the colony amicably and eventually became publisher of *Christianity Today* magazine. Suzanne's work has appeared in many magazines, including *Today's Christian Woman, Worldwide Challenge, ParentLife, Christian Parenting Today, Marriage Partnership*, and many others. She has contributed to several nonfiction books and is the author of three novels. Fisher lives with her family in the San Francisco Bay Area.

To Follow Her Heart, Must She Leave the Community She Loves?

The Choice

by SUZANNE FISHER

Don't miss the first novel in the Lancaster County Secrets series, coming January 2010!

Ɍ Revell
a division of Baker Publishing Group
www.RevellBooks.com

Available wherever books are sold.